CROCHET PATTERNS FOR BEGINNERS

THE ULTIMATE GUIDE TO LEARN CROCHETING. TIPS AND TRICKS TO CREATE YOUR FAVORITE PATTERNS.

PENELOPE COLE

Table of contents

INTRODUCTION

Crochet is a way to make yarn or crochet thread with a crochet hook. In fact, the word crochet means 'hook.'

You just start your project with a slip knot, insert the crochet hook through the latch, wrap yarn through the hook, and pull it around the first latch. Keep on wrapping the fleece over the hook and get them through the last one loop until the ideal length is reached. Through loop is known as a chain, since it goes through the past loop.

When this chains are creating, it is possible to join the last sequence with a slip knot to form a circle and run-in rounds, or it is possible to turn the chains and work in rows. If you work through rows, you become the job at the end of and row, but when you operate in rounds, you have enough choice to turn or not. The patterns let you know when and when they won't transform.

Once the yarn is wrapped around the ring, and one or even more loops are pulled via the chain or from the previous row or circle. The best thing about crochet is that only one active loop remains at the end of each thread.

You can make all sorts of clean fabrics like doilies, bedspreads, table cloths, and afghans with crochet. You can make your own clothing, including sweaters, headbands, ponchos, scarves, tops, caps, slippers. You may also crochet other items like bags, dishcloths, mats, and napkins.

Patterns usually tell you what yarn and what crochet hook size to use. Thick yarn requires a bigger crochet hook, whereas thin thread or crochet thread is handled with a relatively small hook.

Starting to learn how to crochet can be difficult; the yarn needs to be kept on one side, and the crochet hook on the other, and both must work together to achieve the completed project. Crocheting can take a lot of time for people who just learn to crochet, but with regular practice, speed is increased. It can even be stressful at first, but ultimately it is really soothing when one is one of the yarns and hooks and can also relieve tension.

CHAPTER ONE

What Is Crocheting?

Although crocheting isn't around as long as the old knitting art, it's been a revival in popularity like other crafts. The first proof of crochet was not until the 19th century, as before, when people used to build cloth using more economical techniques. In comparison to sewing, crocheting has evolved to give females luxuries such as lace curtains, collars, and more. Today the latest look of crochet is as latest fabrics, hooks, and yarns are common.

Crochet varies from other sewing and stitching styles. Although knitting loops and long needles, crocheting is a form of needlework with a crochet needle that uses a hooked needle to lock one thread loop. Hooks are made of aluminum or stainless steel in all sizes and shapes. The size and shape of the hook influences the thread, and the yarn size also determines the size of the hook.

Like knitting, crochet depends on simple stitches and adjustments in simple stitches. Four essential stitches are available. First of all, there is single crochet, the shortest point, a substantial, and flat impact. The other three main stitches are double hooks, triple crochet, and half-double hooks. Crocheting starts with a single thread, a cross-stitched row with all stitches and successive rows.

The type of crochet yarn selected will significantly influence the finished product. Although there is no yarn standard, yarns range from lightweight, like the ones used for baby clothes to bulky or extra bulky yarns, which are suitable for teapots. Wool yarn is a good yarn, to begin with, because it is stretchable, and silk is the right choice, although it is cheaper. When following a pattern, it is essential that you work on the correct gage of the pattern so that you can correctly replicate the pattern. Suggested hook size is usually recommended to help you retain the same size. But you can still make a swatch first.

Crochet learning can be enjoyable and engaging. Although some terms and equipment are required for any project, it does not have to be unnecessarily complicated. Crochet is also suitable for small projects that can be completed in a few days and for more complex creations. If you want a soothing craft, crocheting can be worthwhile.

Crocheting will allow you to do a lot from small sacks to jackets and sweaters. There are various options available. Crochet pattern publishers also search for pattern testers. Contact several companies and deliver trends for analysis. Crochet patterns produced by Chinese manufacturers with excellent production and the most affordable prices. Lists will rightly lead you to vital data like company category, essential items, target audience, contact information, certifications, and more, for example.

Crotchetier does not exclusively restrict himself to the pattern instructions. It is necessary to exercise a personal opinion, which will enhance the appearance of the project. These guides are most helpful for hobby-news, but crochet patterns can also be used by experienced experts. Crocheting will allow you to do a lot from small sacks to jackets and sweaters. There are various options available. Crochet pattern publishers also search for pattern testers. Crochet patterns produced by Chinese manufacturers with excellent production and the most affordable prices.

In addition to the traditional knitting lessons, several more new pattern books are printed, with modern designs, and most yarn stores also sell crochet lessons. Filets crochet, broomstick lace, hairpin lace, Tunisian crochet, cro-hooking, and Irish crochet are all variations of the traditional crochet process. The magazines most frequently feature simple crochet patterns built for beginners and even crocheters. Expert Crotchetier, who designs the patterns commonly featured in art magazines for a long, long time.

Anyone who does crochet will tell you that creating and producing a range of beautiful and completely original items with their own two hands is totally invaluable. For beginners, the first pillow, first scarf, first table cover carries with it happiness previously unknown.

And giving away crochet Christmas stuff is just one of many beautiful ideas for crochet. All crochet projects start with a knot of slip. Place the end of the yarn over your palm from right to left with the palm of your hand facing you and back to cross over your palm again and place it over the end of the first yarn pole.

Expert crocheter who crochet the designs featured mostly in art magazines for a long time. Now place the yarn over the crochet thread, insert and pull it in the last loop. That's how you begin any crochet project. When putting a flat, it looks like a big crocheted pattern with a hole in the middle. This is a quick and basic crocheted Afghan cover, a perfect gift for family and friends. It can be used as a cover or shawl in cold nights as a blanket. The problem of choosing the correct size or color window accents can be easily avoided by using crochet window accent templates so that shopping time can be saved. The specific design or style required for your decoration may not always be commercially available, but you can always find a pattern that works or can be adjacent with a little imagination by using crocheted window accents.

A wide range of free and commercial crochet patterns covering a wide variety of applications are available. Changes in fashion mean that various types of crocheted items are common during different periods. If you're new to wire crocheting, try not to crochet too close; let the wire pass freely through your fingers. Without careful preparation, bead crochet bags could be made and include more freeform technologies. Knitted and crocheted pieces continued to be accessible at the beginning of 1900? s. Whether it's a Halloween suit for the little one or a holiday table runner, you can also get free crochet patterns from crochet magazines, art journals, and libraries. But the internet tends to be a viable choice, as all your free habits can be accomplished by sitting at home. These guides are most helpful for hobby-news, but crochet patterns can also be used by experienced experts. Some suggest that a crochet or knitting bag could be a good step in keeping your things organized and contained. But you should probably wait until your supplies and set actually go.

Crochet Stitches Basic

The chain stitch, the plip-stitch, the double crochet stitch, and the triple stitch are among the common crochet stitches. Be confident and able to make these stitches is essential since most crochet patterns include them all. Also, you can find designs that either skip the triple or the double of crochet stitch, so this is vital that you get one at least such simple stitch. However, it's not long before you feel the need to include them in the arsenal of your crochet skills.

To start crocheting, it is necessary to start from the starting position. It is gained by bowing the yarn in a looped ring and inserting the hake into the loop and as well catching the thread with your hand, and then returning it to the looped ring and then tightening the node on your hand. The next step is to keep the crochet hook in your usual dominant hand in a manner that is comfortable for you (such as a pen or a knife) and keep the yarn tightly underneath the slip knot.

The stitching of the chain is the first stitches crochet used in any pattern, providing either a circular or straight-line crochet with the baseline or ring. It is a fundamental stitch in crochet patterns abbreviated as ch.

Wrap your yarn around your thread (two laps on a loop) and pull it through the first lap on its shaft to operate a number of chain stitches. Now you have only one hook loop, and a chain stitch has been developed. Repeat this cycle for as many chain points as appropriate for your particular pattern or project.

You need to tie the chain stitches together with a slip stitch when crocheting in the round (circular clothes like caps, padlocks, and squares are made this way). A slip stitch in crochet patterns is shortened toss. This is quite clear. Place the crochet hook into the center of the first crocheted chain stitch, gather the yarn then draw the hook out and put two loops on the hook again. Then draw the hook into the first loop on the hook and leave just a single loop on the hook.

The abbreviated of double crochet stitch is DC, or the single crochet stitch in America is very similar to the one mentioned above. However, the hook is put in the next thread. This depends on what project you are doing. After putting the thread, take the yarn and draw the crochet back from stitch, leaving the two loops on the handle. Lace the yarn around hook more time to make three-line loops. At last, draw the hook through all the circles to leave the one loop on the crochet with a double crochet thread.

The last basic crochet stitch that we deal with is the triple stitch, which is abbreviated in crochet patterns and known in America as the double crochet. This is the toughest of the simple crochet stitches, and the meat and vegetables of crochet since this stitch is based on many advanced stitches and techniques. It is also a good idea to execute this crochet stitch effectively.

Wrap the yarn around the hook before putting your hook into the stitch you want your treble to stand in, to crochet a triple stitch. Catch the thread and take the hook out of the loop. You'll have three loops on your hook at this stage. Wrap the yarn through your hook again and make four-thread loops. Now pull the hook over the second and third loops on the hook and leave you on your hook with two loops. Loop the yarn through the hook again and draw the hook via these remaining loops, leave you on the hook with only one loop and a triple made.

You now have the basic crochet methods, as we discussed the simple crochet stitches. You 're shocked how many patterns and projects with this small amount of crocheting information are now available. Please don't just take my word and look for yourself! And remember, have fun! And remember!

History of The Crochet

Nobody really knows when or how to crochet was initially being made. This is due to the fact that the unlike knitting, crochet, was more the needle art in comparison to the intricate lace knitting crafted for royalty and the high class which was then preserved for research by museums and historians.

Over the years, crochet has stayed true to its origins and was always a more affordable and flexible handy than knitting and to make more creative and decorative clothing, Afghans, hats, and other projects.

Historians accept that crochet was invented by the classes that is lower. It's difficult to trust now, but fine yarns and knitting needles and threads were accessible only to the very wealthy in early history. That left everybody who was weak and wanted a lucky hobby. And when such products were made available to a growing middle class in Europe, it was only intended to knit darn socks.

An unrecorded underground crochet movie only began with people who found some kind of strands or threads and used their fingers to create decorative knots and chains. This initial attempt may have been closer than crochet to macramé, but has still become a cheap and imaginative art for the masses.

In Turkey, Persia, China, North Africa, and India, people possibly started to fashion hooks out from either metal, bone, ivory, or wood around the 1300s. But before people really began "rising in the air," as it was later called in France in the 1800s, a different way of knotting and looping threads was first developed.

Since nobody realized that the crochet stitch could create a garment on its own, it switched to a process called 'tambourine.' The process was established first in China and required crochet-like stitches made of cloth. Around 1700, textile makers stretched a backdrop taught to a frame and then used a needle with a hook to move a thread loop through the tissue. When the next loop was made, the catch was combined, and the first chain point was made.

By the middle to the end of the 1700s, many of the first bits of tambourine had entered Europe from the East, in order to encourage Europeans to learn to drum for themselves. The cloth was eventually removed, and the top-class Europeans, who perfected the art of drumming, started to create the first modern crochet with hooks made from brass, silver, and steel. Again, of course, as it was only the high-ranking class who could crochet, masses were left to darn socks and dream of more creative outlets.

It just takes some time before the people learned to design their own hooks and get a hold of odds and ends of the film to accent their own clothes. (When first in Europe, crochet was not used to create entire garments, as it was used for decorating existing clothes.)

The upper class, which made crochet fashionables, saw, and instantly proclaimed the emerging middle class and their new crochet. They soon returned to the knitting cycle that the lower levels could not afford and did not come back to crochet until Queen Victoria picked up her crochet and made it fashionable.

A more modern crochet variant originated from Italy and Spain, but it was in 1700 that the French developed crochet, calling it "croche" "croc," or which means " the hook," from the Middle French word. By 1842, the French also came up with the first clothing patterns. Crocheted lace was also produced during this time.

Later, uniform patterns were circulated, which were easy to follow. Even though it took time to create standardized needles, by the mid-1800's crochet became the most affordable way for the rising middle class to spend time in the kitchen, while at the same time making unique garments, decorations, and accessories.

Modern crochet remains the people's needles to this day. It is easy to learn, enjoyable to do, and much less restrictive than its more difficult knitting relative. In fact, something called 'random crocheting' is one of the most experienced crocheters.

Simple crocheting is the practice of taking and modifying a template to create your own original version. You can even begin crocheting with an idea and just see what 's going on. That's the beauty of crochet and what makes it so satisfactory, beautiful, and calming in this incredibly modern as well as fast-paced environment.

CROCHETING EARLY TIMES

Hooked tapestries are one of the early American crafts made by women who have to find ways of using any piece of material they have or can handle. The crocheted and woven the long pieces of fabric into teapots and put the shorter sections into hooked teapots. Hooks and yarns are easy to tell from our mother or even our grandmothers, but they are also very cheap, and you can get in any of the major craft shops.

The main reason you will need to buy the entire yarn for the project you will be making is that because of the dyes, the color changes, and you just want to do the project, you undoubtedly wish to all the color to be equal? The craft store reveals that both hooks and needle sizes are labeled with letters, numbers, or millimeters (mm) on the needle's shaft. Once you obtain a new pattern before beginning a project, the instructions indicate precisely what crochet hook size or needle size is appropriate for the pattern.

Lacks back in the old days were very costly to purchase, and people turned to crochet to make a less expensive garment for themselves. Crocheting never needed a lot of machinery and other materials, and all people of all ages learned to crochet for themselves to make fine laces.

Some of the main issues with some laces are that it is usually very thin and crumpled and rough until pinned to its maximum expected size and shape. In the past day, a lot of people would have taken the time to block the pieces on bed towels or floors in a space, but today you'll want to invest in a blocking board for your shopping if you're going to make many items that require blocking. You can find them in your nearest art store.

We have ever thought this would be the first Eve and Adam to decorate, cover, and clothe themselves and their houses. Most people may not know how to treat wool items or other natural fibers.

Crochet thread was used for both designs until the early '50s. Many people, particularly the younger generation, had begun to practice crochet for themselves at that time. With the introduction of colored yarns, many new designs and ideas were created that caused an explosion of numerous designs and patterns, and many different colors in the crochet arena.

There is also another method called Felting for Crotchetier. This is to carry out good long-term ventures. The felting process is used to make wool fibers and tighten them into a dense, sturdy material, incredibly durable and long-lasting.

Many of our early cultures have used felt wool during their travels to construct their shelters. Felting is what occurs when a favorite wool sweater gets mistakenly washed, and we know what happens; then, it looks like something. Should your grandchild wear properly? You should not use dyed wool with felting, which means the wool is not like yarn.

WHERE IS CROCHET FROM AND WHEN?

I know of several of the most widely used crochet types called Crochet, in the West, including many methods using crochet stitches and yarns and loops; stitches with names such as chain stitch, slip stitch, double crochet stitch, half and treble and one and more.
Archeological findings suggest that Arabia is the first place where a needle or hook is made of fiber. Old samples from Egypt indicate skilled use of needles and hooks from 950BC – 1200BC.

Over time, crochet is a term from the French word croc, meaning cord, and is considered to have been employed by men and women. A technique that can be produced sitting, standing, lying or while on the move, using a variety of yarn, silk, cotton, linen, and wool, including precious metals finely spun or spun (in silver or gold), with or without beads and spangles; to make cloths, stones, containers, rugs, sheets, furniture fabrics, light clothing, and t Similar crochet patterns that have been found in India and North Africa testify to the hypothesis that crochet has been used for thousands of years in the Middle East.

If it is an afghan or tricot crochet, Tunisian crochet worked with what looks like a cross between crochet and a needle, where and when did it surface? Was that Tunisia? Was it the first runner of each of those ways of making crochet that can look like crochet or knitting or weaving?

Slip crochet stitch, probably the earliest type of crochet and textiles.

Broom crochet sometimes called peacock lace, when and where did it come from? Was it created by Europeans traveling in covered wagons through America, they had broomsticks and hooks, they had the expertise they had, they took them out of their homeland, they needed hot bedding and clothes, did they start making the crochet quickly and easily?

Irish crochet, traditional Irish crochet, luxury 3-D lace characteristic of a network of chain stitches with picots (called, the fillings), feminine, lovely, and romantic. A subgroup of Irish crochet often referred to as Irish baby crochet is continuously working on squares or circular pieces. Crochet was the salvation of many Irish families in the 1870s when 12,000 to 20,000 Irish girls and women made crochet lace to raise money to support their families over and beyond potato famine years.

Bruges Crochet, a lace made out of triples and chain stitch, the crochet ribbons are joined together to create a clear tape like lace.

Bavarian Crochet, new to me, this regional crochet needs to know more.

Aran crochet is like Aran knitting, shapes a cloth that is flat with elevated regions.

Fillet crochet or net crochet was trendy in the 1920-1950s, popular with users because of its simple mesh design and lace design.

Hairpin crochet is thought to have been developed in Queen Victorian times by ladies using their pins and hooks to create a new crochet design used in fine linen and round laces, to make it better for polishing. Today we have replaced the bolts with looms that are modified in size to make this crochet type easier to function.

Revival in the swinging 60s as individuals decided to work modern style garments, by hand, in inconsistent form and color, to the day's standards.

Stripes, jacquards, patchworks, knit, laces, looped, beaded, triangles, woven, circles today crumbling, crochet is a living art, reviving, re-inventing and using new fabrics in ways that look infinite. How people across history and around the world have satisfied their own personal needs, earned money, fed their families, dressed themselves and their families, production of new goods, and fulfilling their desire to do so.

Crochet at the beginning of the 21st century saw a new resurgence in manufacturing, creating and finding thousands of fashion and decorative items in the hands of individuals, developing new designs and technologies, handmade decorative pieces, personal garments, and artworks.
Crochet patterns continue to evolve, and Crochet continues to live on.

Guide on Crochet Stitch

Test this crochet stitch guide for the most common crochet stitches. Such stitches are crochet building blocks. Once you learn to crochet, you first master those stitches before you switch to the patterns.

A pattern point consists of organized stitches, repeatedly creating patterns, shells, clusters, and decorative motifs. You use models to make crocheted things like scarves, hats, baby blankets, etc.

You will learn how to personalize a written pattern with various crochet hooks or yarns. A pattern of the stitch can be as simple as two or twelve rows. You will keep track of where you are by a row counter.

Stitches for Performance Crochet

Texture crochet patterns render a multitude of lightweight designs using simple crochet stitches.

The alternate stitch is made for turning by a series of two chains plus two. Begin by making the chain the length you need, turn it and make two single hooks in the next chain (or stitch, on subsequent rows) after skipping the three chains (chain turning). Then skip a string and a chain. Then skip chain. Repeat to make the two single hooks in the last thread, chain two, and switch to the previous loop. The second-row creates the two crochet points in the unique string and skips and chains in the last row over the two crochets. Those two rows form a pattern that looks like a leaf when it is written.

The two stitches are identical to the alternating stitch, but they cover two stitches instead of having two single crochets in one row. Please insert your crochet hook in the thread, wrap the yarn over it and then take out the hook and insert it into the next thread. Yarn over so that you take an extra loopback and pull the yarn on the hook through all three loops. Repeat the double stitch on each pair of row stitches. This pattern makes a warm baby blanket with soft, washable crochet yarn.

Many stitches with thickness include:

- Up to Down, with single and double stitches alternating.

- Checker pattern board created with three or four single and double crochet stitches in alternating classes.

- Woven stitching made in chain stitches by crocheting one single crochet, chaining one, missing the next stitch, and then hooking another single crochet. Replay this over the first row and crochet one in the previous row 's chain area, skip and chain one over the individual hooks in the initial rows.

Stitch diagonal, using long stitches taken from three single or double crochet stitches in groups.

Many more texture stitches are available. When you've tried a few, you will start to come up with your own textures.

Stitches for Shell or Fan Pattern

Some of the most common designs for baby blankets, litters, and afghans are the shell or fan point. A shell is a set of three to five points that have been cut into one piece of chain. The group is closer together on the bottom and stretches upwards so that every group appears like a fan or a seashell.

A plain shell has double crochet in a single thread, then two double hooks, a single chain, and another two double hooks in the next thread. The next stitch makes another double crochet, but the loop is carried over three skips, and a smaller fan is made. Each big shell is stitched into the stitch underneath the shell and provides a punched bottom.

Shell variations can be created by crocheting low shells in the narrow chain spaces, making an open, delicate pattern suitable for clothing and blankets for children. You can create an arch-like pattern by making large shells in public areas. Have a fan open up over an opening, and you'll have a lovely starburst design.

Crochet Stitch Patterns Cluster

Perhaps the most common cluster point is the bobble stitch. The bobbles are usually created by turning a yarn over, putting the hook into the base stitch of the bobble, and pulling a loop out. Then you make another thread and pull the thread through two of the hook stitches. This is repeated five times in the base stitch, which means that six loops remain on the hook. The yarn pulled by all the six loops to form the pin and fixed in the following stitch by creating single crochet.

The pineapple stitch is another typical cluster pattern. Operated on a multiple of two plus four, the apple is made with a yarn over, a crochet hook is inserted in a single thread, and four times it is drawn up, and the yarn is over. Draw the eight loops of crochet yarn, then make another yarn and pull the yarn through the last two loops. In comparison to bobbles, pineapples typically are not grounded with single crochet stitches. Alternatively, a stitch is sprung between each an apple, and over the skipped stitch, a chain is made. In the next row, the ananas is made in the chain between the ananas of the last row. The top of the apple is skipped, and a string is placed over it.

You will have a better understanding of how the simple crochet stitches can be made. Find some crochet books, browse the internet, and then consider making some of your own designs.

CROCHET ART

By the early 1800s, fabrics made from lace were much more expensive than crochet goods. Some communities in Europe use crochet products to identify their social status, which only indicates their ability to afford crochet products and other lace products. The art of crocheting requires only cheaper tools and materials, usually threads and yarns that can be purchased in nearby markets.

Some claim that crocheting and knitting have developed in countries such as China, Saudi Arabia, and Brazil. This hypothesis has been established due to the cultural pattern of clothes used by the people living in these countries. Many experts also say that crocheting is more critical than its necessity to create crochet and knitted products to bend the forefinger.

During the early years of imperialism, when art was practiced during Western Europe, crocheting was regarded as the primary tool of people living in villages and communities. Most royalties suggest using a crochet product to reflect wealth and strength. Crocheting and knitting are the joy of many people these days. It has grown as an artist to make very well-designed crochet crafts.

An individual may purchase a range of threads and yarns for the creation of a crochet product. Based on the type of pattern or design you may make, there are different textures and colors. There are actually specific forms of yarn on the market. He may find baby/fingering, baby/sport, worsted weight, and lightweight yarn styles, primarily used in crocheting and knitting.

Yarns are usually labeled for the consistency of yarns according to their styles. It helps to decide which specific thread is suitable for a particular crochet product. A person may also need to know the quantity of the skein, instructions for care, gauge, and fiber of the yarns.

Below are some other materials, apart from the yarn, required to make a particular crochet product.

1. The knitting needles are also useful for crocheting. These are typically straight materials of metal, wood, and plastic. We can be found in various sizes between 2 mm and 15 mm. They are purchased in pairs with a button and pointing tops. This design was designed to prevent the needle from slipping on the unfinished crochet product.

2. The crochet hooks are used to hold crochet thread loops. We often derive the loosening and slipping stitches from the chain stitches. They are also made of titanium, plastic, and wood. The wooden crochet hooks are the most popular crochet items because they are simpler to handle and, therefore, the most affordable.

3. The pattern diagram is fundamental to construct a crochet product. This is the guide to following the directions and the concept description. Most patterns are generally easy to follow, mainly if the person is very competent in crocheting. For most beginners, models are more comfortable and more precise. We are specifically designed to learn and appreciate basic crochet items designs.

4. He will also need to use other tools to provide him with sufficient simple crochet instructions such as magazines and books and diagrams that he can use if he decides to select a particular way of making a crochet pillow, crochet hat, crochet bag, crochet scarf, etc.

5. Different supplies are also needed in the production of varying crochet items. Lace made, and doilies must be worked on with hooks in stainless steel. Such special hooks have a different size than standard wooden hooks.

Crochet goods are often crafted to make beautiful patterns. These can be shown in exhibitions in particular if the equipment and supplies used are crochet materials approved. The quality of the crochet product will also depend on how long an individual has made it. Although many work only on crochet goods for their own enjoyment and pleasure, people often find it useful to apply their skills to generate income.

Different faces of the yarn fibers

The oldest known examples of yarn and cloth of any kind are near Robenhausen in Switzerland, which is believed to be around 7,000 years old by bundles of flax fibers and thread and pieces of basic weaves.

Browsing the yarn section of craft shops, there seems to be regular discontinuation of various yarn fibers and the addition of new ones.

To beginners, the selection of yarn fibers, such as acrylic, alpaca, radius, etc., without adequate knowledge of their material is difficult. You can make choices of yarn from a yarn fiber based on the criteria that are eco-friendly, animal-free, and vegan friendly.

This will include some detail on the various crochet and knitting fibers, which are classified as a natural, plant, and synthetic.

Animal Fiber Yarn.

Alpaca – A more beautiful fiber made from alpaca fleece, a South American animal domesticated. It's softer, lighter, and more cumbersome than wool and colder. Moreover, organic alpaca yarn has started to be added to the yarn industry.

Cashmere- An excellent synthetic fiber originating from the thick fleecy undergrowth of Tibet's Cashmere horse, Iraq, China, Mongolia, Iran, and India. Cashmere is harvested by combing rather than cutting from the cow. This is most commonly found in dresses, sweaters, jackets, shawls, and shoes.

Llama fiber-Made out of a double-coated, mammalian Llama skin. It's beautiful, downy undercoat protects against heat and cold. The second coat of crimp-free safe hair allows moisture and waste to be removed. The wool is surprisingly warm and soft, rains and snow are eliminated and comes in a range of colors. Contrary to sheep fur, during washing or processing, it shrinks less.

Possum- Among the new yarns launched on the market for the thread. It was developed from the brushtail possessions of New Zealand, first introduced in 1858 from Australia. The appearance of a big cat with a fluffy, luxurious fur is a nightmarish marsupial. Possum wool yarn is a truly luxurious yarn with all the features other yarn fibers provide. Feels like cashmere; hard to wear, lighter and more relaxed in winter than wool and in summer.

Silk-This is one of man's oldest woven fibers. The Chinese have been using it since the 27th century BC. The silk fiber is produced in the form of cocoons by silkworms. Silk is durable, flexible, and fibrous. Silk absorbs humidity that makes it cool in summer and warm in winter. It is easily colored in many deep colors due to its high absorption. Silk does not shrink like other fabrics Silk maintains its form, clothes well and shrinks with all its own luster.

Fiber Yarn Factory.

Bamboo – originated from bamboo – a woody group of perennial evergreen plants in the specific Poaceae family of grass. A Wikipedia notice notes that Bamboo is remarkable for its smooth feel and evidence of natural antibacterial properties. Bamboo fiber clothing is famous for activities such as yoga.

Cotton-Fine silky cotton fabrics in their raw state from cotton plants. This is used in materials, absorbs and retains moisture, is easy to wash, and is available in several different forms and qualities. There is also organic cotton yarn available on the market. Usually, for baby projects like blankets, scarves, and caps, you can use organic cotton yarn.

Rayon-One of the world's oldest man-made fabric. Rayon is not plastic, unlike other man-made fibers. This is made of wood pulp, a natural raw material dependent on cellulose. This fiber of cellulose is easily absorbed. The durability and coloring ability are excellent and very soft. Rayon continues to decrease but does not melt at high temperatures. This is moth resistant and is not harmed by ordinary bleaches and chemicals in the household. It's used in apparel, draperies, tapestries, and bedding

The fiber of synthetic fibers.

Acrylic-A man-made of cloth, not wool or cloth of a plant. It is a synthetic fiber that is fast-drying. It is also cheaper than other strands of the yarn. The acrylic fiber can be used to create any project. If these products are clothing, they cannot be as long-lasting because of the lack of elasticity.

Corn-is a synthetic fiber no-oil. The new, environmentally friendly fiber produced by the Cargill Dow Company is also called PLA (Poly Lactic Acid) and mostly produced as ingo maize fiber on the market. This uses lactic acid as raw materials from starch, which is entirely reasonable and of biodegradability. Thanks to their n-oil content, microbial waste can be dissolved, and no environmental contamination caused by carbon dioxide and water in the soil.

LYCRA-This is an elastic fiber produced by humans. This has exceptional stretch and recovery properties, rarely used alone, but slightly blended together with other fibers. LYCRA Fiber allows knitwear designers to make trendy and added value sweaters: outstanding shape retention, simple care, and better adaptation.

Microfiber-The smallest man-made fiber ever produced is a microfiber. A modern, excellent polyester fiber that narrowly doubles the look and feel of natural fibers. Microfiber fabrics are wrinkle-resistant and easy to treat.

Olefin – This is a synthetic alkene fiber. It is used in the production of various textiles as well as in the manufacturing of furniture, wallpaper, garments, cables, and interior vehicles.

The fiber offers weightless energy. The fibers are absorbed by low moisture, but can quickly dry and dry up. Olefin fiber is resistant to abrasion, stain, sunlight, and chemical.

I encourage beginners to use acrylic yarn because it is inexpensive and readily available. As our skills and projects expand, the choices of yarn fibers change over time.

CHAPTER TWO

Crochet for Beginners

And you thought you are going to know how to crochet. You probably already know you won't be able to read a single post and learn everything you need to know. After reading this book, however, you will be ready to start learning crochet well. Even when you finish this book, you can learn more about learning what you need to know about crocheting.

What you need to know first is crochet. Crocheting is the method by which a thread or yarn material is produced with a crochet hook. You can pick from an infinite difference of threads, yarns, and many hook styles. You pull thread loops of yarn through other loops to create the textiles. It probably sounds easy, we know. The reality is that it is. The point is that you need skill and dexterity to do it correctly. The right hooks, yarn, and instructions are also required. You have to ensure that you do it correctly, or else you end up with something unusable rather than your own artwork.

A significant aspect of crocheting is to always pick projects with clearly written instructions. If you have written recently, you will have a guide to follow that makes it all easier. If you have proper guidelines, you'll have the answer to a variety of questions like what crochet type to use, what thread type, and where to use the correct stitches. Too many people believe that, rather than following simple directions, they can just improvise and end up with a catastrophe. Such people are disappointed and hope that in the first place, they have done something differently.

You will possibly also see how vital the instructions are to learn how crucial the essential crochet words are. Crochet instructions are typically written using abbreviations and shorthands. Examples of this are DC, meaning double stitch, and SC, meaning single stitch. You will see if you don't know these, that you eventually chase your tail, and wonder what the heck you got into.

One common question beginner ask is what is the difference between knitting and crochet. There's a quick reply. You use two hooks when you knit and only use one when you crochet. This is because you only have one active pin on the hook when you crochet, and you have a whole set of active pins when you knit. That means that losing a stitch when you knit is a total catastrophe, but it doesn't even matter a big deal in crochet. If you know how to crochet, some stuff can make your crocheting experience easier and more enjoyable. There are also some other tools, in addition to hooks and yarns, that you should consider having before you start a crochet project. With all in place at the outset, you can feel much more prepared.

First of all, the sort of hooks or hooks you would use. Crochet hooks consist of different materials, including brass, steel, plastic, or bone. The critical requirements for working with a hook are that you feel confident and relaxed. The weight of your catch, the hook material, the size and length of your finger will influence your decision. There are no clear criteria for choosing a hook, but it is essential to consider how tight or lose you crochet. Of course, if you follow a pattern, then you must be aware of the measuring specifications of how many stitches you need to make an inch.

Buying an Afghan hook might be a smart investment. Afghan hooks are used for special crochet projects and can keep a lot of stitches on your needle. The crochet hook is six inches on average, but Afghan hooks are 9, 14, and 20-inch long. They also have sticks on them to keep the stitches in place. Using an Afghan hook makes it much easier to crochet.

Yarns are now available for crochet use in several different varieties. As a beginner, a medium or close twist with a smooth surface is the more comfortable yarn to use. Crochet yarn is typically packed as balls and not as skeletal, and the length of each yarn depends on the thickness. You will want to find an all-natural mix, or you may obtain a combination of both of them when you look at synthetic yarns that are both natural and synthetic.

There are other devices in addition to yarn and hooks that make crocheting easier. Markers are split loops or colorful plastic circles that help to mark the work. You contribute to demonstrate the start of a row and to count the stitches. Tapestry needles are used for gripping but can be used for crocheting in the spinning of yarn ends and stitching crochet bits together.

There are more devices you can use once you start crocheting, but getting the above on hand will make it much easier for you to crochet. It is also easier to prepare the materials that you need in advance so that in the middle of a job, you are not interrupted. Soon, you'll be one-of-a-kind crafts crocheting.

All right, you want to know about crocheting.

So, what exactly is crocheting? It is a way to create fabric out of thread or yarn with a device called a crochet hook. There are several different threads and yarns on the market and large amounts of various hooks. Crochet works by pulling thread or yarn loops into a set of neighboring loops. It could sound easy, and it really is. However, to do it well, you need some talent and ability. You must also have the correct yarns, hooks, and guides. Like anything else, if you're not careful, you can end up messing your hard work from the beginning.
The key to tasty crochet is to make sure you select a project with proper instructions. If you do this, you will find it so much easier. This is because you have clear guidance, such as the best yarn and hook to use, and how to make the correct stitches. Many people assume that they can just dive in without the right direction, and the end result isn't great!

Instructions are necessary, and it is crucial that you first know all the fundamentals of crocheting. Many instructions use abstract words like DC for double crochet and SC for single crochet, etc. If you do not know these terms and conditions, you will not understand the instructions at all, and your tests will be wrong.

Many people wonder how different crocheting and knitting are. The answer is easy. The use of 2 hooks is required for knitting, while crochet only requires one. Since crocheting has only one point that is active, whereas knitting involves a number of active points in a row when you knit a thread, it may mean the end of the project, but it's not a disaster with crochet.

More details can be found in my signature. Here you can find a sample of an excellent tool that teaches you everything you ever need to learn about crochet.

Tips for starting

Crochet is a skill that takes time and consideration to develop and master. Like any skill, some basics will make it easier for beginners to learn crochet. This book's aim is to provide beginners with information that will help you learn how to crochet.

1-Crochet stitches are everything. This is the most fundamental aspect. There are so many stitches to master, and some stitches are known by different names depending on where you live. The first tip is to learn the stitch of the chain. This is the simplest way to practice and forms the basis for all the other stitches.

2-The right size of the hook. It is necessary to select the appropriate hook size for the product you are making. Choose your pattern and get the right hook for the yarn you want to send the right thread for your pattern. The "lease" is the number of stitches per inch. And the number of stitches you get per inch is entirely dependent upon your hook size and the yarn diameter. The that, of course, the fewer stitches you get to the inch. The pattern advises you to use the gauge, and you only have to use the correct size needle and yarn to give you the measure.

3-Carefully pick your thread. The yarn you choose must suit the pattern you make. You need to know the type of fiber of the yarn, the thickness or weight of the yarn, and whether or not it suits your budget. Ideally, you would buy all the yarn needed to complete the pattern concurrently and make sure it comes from the same stock so that when finished, there is no color difference.

Crochet Designing for Beginners

For several years, crochet patterns have been made. It has recently become a phenomenon in the fashion world again. The person will indeed be able to come up with some fantastic designs to show people by studying about it.

This is better to continue with the essential elements when people start something original. It is almost all, and crochet patterns are no different. If the individual has cross-stitched in the past, it is easy to see how some designs are made. If you have no previous experience, you better sign up for a class after a while, you can continue to crochet styles.

The world of fashion is a perfect place to learn more about crochet designs. Since this is determined by some of the world's renowned brands, learning from these experts will keep the consumer up-to-date. Fashion usually reveals the next clothes a few months before it is launched. Once you see the fabric studied after it hits the stores, you can create a comparable template that is also ready for fresh and hot items.

If the person cannot get the show, the next place to know is in reference materials such as books and videos, which can be purchased in the local specialty shop. It will require all the materials to be used. Many TV shows and magazines can be bought, which feature some of the simples to advanced designs. The person must simply understand and work on the instructions given.

Basics can only be achieved with one light. The individual should do this in making a simple object like a towel. If this works, it can start moving on to bigger stuff.

One of the essentials in making crochet patterns is a slipknot. The person does not have to wear a needle and work with his hands. While one end is around your fingers, you can throw the yarn ball into the air.

After making a few loops, the individual makes a knot using both hands.

Among the challenges in crochet patterns is to move from one color to another. This can be done if one color is stopped, and a different color thread is slowly slid into the needle.

Mixing is another simple technique that the person should master. It is achieved with two needles with different thread colors. When facing each other and letting one of the needles work over the other, the print becomes multi-colorful.

Another technique used to render crochet patterns is a purl stitch. This is very much like mixing. The yarn is around one needle already. The individual then uses the other to work inside before the two can work together to create a pattern.

Cross-stitching is very difficult and will take a lot of work. After some basics are practiced, the individual can make numbers, forms, lines, and others to make them stand out.

The person must remember that the fashion industry passes through the seasons. This means that the person will operate rapidly so that it can still be used in due course once completed. Beginners should be able to draw on paper and examine how a specific concept will be carried out. By using this as a reference, the individual may track the work progress.

Crochet patterns on almost everything can be made. The skills of the person in crochet patterns have improved significantly by working on some small household products and then moving on to clothes, accessories, and accessories.

DO YOU WISH TO LEARN HOW TO CROCHET?

Have you been talking about crochet learning? Many people told me they 'd love to crochet only, but they think it'd be too hard for them to learn. You don't know anything about yarn, hooks, or even how to start.

Honestly, crochet isn't hard at all. It's complicated only if you believe it's, so you have to change your mind by looking at the basic concepts of crochet.

Have you ever seen kids play a yarn or a loop (or maybe you did this yourself)? They create a slip knot with their fingers in the yarn or string, then create a circle and pass it through the first loop, followed by another loop. That's the same thing.

As the original starting crochet thread, except that you are using a crochet hook rather than your fingers.

Where do you pick your yarn? There are five common styles of yarn to choose from: baby/fingering, baby/sports weight, used, chunky, and bulky. For a beginner, worsted weight is the right sort.

Fingering and child's yarn are very fine, usually with three folds (ply refers to the number of strands to form the yarn that is twisted together). The weight of the worn is a 4-ply yarn. Heavier yarns are chunky and bulky.

Yarns may be made of natural or synthetic fibers. Acrylics are conventional and straightforward to use

Clean. Cotton threads are very easy to work with and are an easy project for beginners to produce large crocheted cloths.

You want to stay away from the fur and fuzzy yarns for a beginner. They 're soft and soft.

Very pretty, but harder to work with because your stitches are difficult to see. You can later try them while improving your crocheting skills.

Only look at the labels to pick your yarn. You 're going to ask what you need to know. A few yarns

Have even free label patterns. You would want to save those in your set of models, also though you don't want to build the item right now. Creating a pattern set for later use is always perfect.

Next, you're going to pick your crochet needle. Aluminum, plastic, wood, or steel hooks can be made. Steal hooks, such as doilies and lace, are tiny and used in excellent work.

You'll know the worn yarn as a beginner so that you want an H (5.00 mm), I (5.5 mm), or J (6.00 mm) crook. You will want to create a set of different hook sizes as you learn how to crochet.

The difficulty we have found is that most beginners work together with the hook and yarn. But practice, like anything, is perfect. It's not long until you get to hang it and get it into the flow.

You should do some workshops before you actually produce an object. Begin to create a chain of 15 to 20 strings. You do this by slipping a knot by wrapping the yarn around your finger and pulling the loop across and placing the slip knot on your hook. Push on the two

Yarn ends to close and change the knot of the break. Then take your yarn from back to front around your thread, catch your yarn with your hand and pull it over your ear. Repeat until 15 to 20 chain stitches are in place.

You'll now use the single crochet (sc) to do your workout. In the second chain (count just two chains away from the hook) from your hook, insert your hook into that chain. Place the yarn over the hook and draw it through the stitch of the thread. Now there are two hook loops.

Take your yarn to your hook and draw it on the hook through both loops. There is always one loop on the line. You completed your first single crochet thread.

Continue to repeat the single crochet stitch to the end of the row. If you started with 20 chains, you would have 19 single stitches of crochet in this row, skip the first chain, and started from your hook in the second chain.

You can make a chain stitch to do your next row of single crochet by wrapping threads over the hook and pulling it on your hook via the loop. You now switch your job so that the last sc you did in the previous row is right at the top. Create a single crochet stitch in the earlier row of each other's thread. For every new line, repeat this.

You'll find that the tops of the completed single crochet stitches have two loops. You bring both of these loops into your anchor. Some beginners make a mistake by only going through a single crochet loop. The variation fits well with specific forms, but then you learn to develop your skills.

Continue to carry out your sample piece before you feel like crocheting. This will help you learn to carry your crochet in a way that makes it easy to pick up the yarn and also helps you to relax. You may find that at first, you crochet too loosely or too tightly. When you practice, you can learn how to manage consistent stress during the project.

When you have practiced and feel like you are ready to try a simple pattern, you can check for a scarf pattern online. Dishcloths are natural patterns for beginners, as mentioned earlier.

I'm sure you'll enjoy your experience with crochet. Consider it soothing, a great relief of tension. It's also fun to work with colors and textures of various yarns. It's fantastic that you can make things for yourself and for family and friends as gifts.

You can do so when watching Television, sitting in a doctor's waiting room or riding in a car as a passenger. Only get a crochet tote bag (or yourself to crochet one), and you're good to go.

Sweater Knit For Beginners

Whenever you want a Sweater knit, you must surely understand how to knit a Sweater 's pattern.

You have to understand the necessary steps prior to actually knitting the sequence:

Take a look

This is where knitting begins, and a cast-on essentially creates loops around the needle.

Line Knit

This is where the knitting project begins to take shape, and knitted rows consist of stitching.

Tie-Off

The big final! The bind is the last part of a knitting project, and you have to remove your project from the needles when the last row of your pattern is done, so binding off is the way you use to go through it.

These are the simple tree stuff that you need to learn to finish any knitting project.

Now, you need a needle for the fabrics you want to knit a Sweater, you can't knit with your hands, of course. And more materials like:

Bulky Yarn: Bulky Yarn

Yarn is the long and continuous thread the people use to knit, crochet, and sew. Why use a spherical yarn? And it's perfect for small projects and more significant projects where you need quick results. The best feature of bulky yarn is straightforward to use, which makes it suitable for beginners.

Holders of Stitch:

Stitch Holders are devices for keeping open stitches if the needles are not used.

When you knit and decide to take a break and start with the project later, a stitch holder must be used. This method is basically used to save a plan then. It is also helpful to recover needles in use if something else is required.

Stitch holders can be used to finish the sweater side and brace for the stitch Kitchener.

Markers Stitch:

The points are small round objects that could be slipped onto the needle knitting to mark a spot in the row. Stitch markers are typically used for circular knitting to mark the end of a string. These can also be make used of to mark increases, decreases, or chains of different stitches.

After you have all the supplies, you still have an essential thing to remember, and you have to get to know some pattern snitches, turn between colors and hold your yarn while you make the sweater.

Different Knitting Stitches Patterns Types:

- Purl and Knit
- Rib Stitches
- Lace and Eyelet
- Stockinette stitch
- Twists and Cables
- Cable knitting stitches
- Garter Stitch
- Moss stitch
- Slip stitches
- Nupps stitches

It's not so hard to knit, and you only need some practice in order to produce lovely creations. It's tough to explain how to knit by word only, but if you find the right training videos, people to talk to or knit with a teacher, it's a lot easier to learn.

Vintage Crochet Patterns For Beginner

Would you like to use vintage crochet structures? Some people want to go through old magazines and see all the uses of crochet hooks and work with yarn, threads, and rags, yes, that is right. We recall the ragman who came to our house for a pound to buy the old clothing. He was holding a scale and charging for the pound.

They seem to have taken longer than personalizing their homes. Not that we're not putting our own personal touches in our homes today, but how often do you find a hot crochet pad in the kitchen today? A finely crocheted table cloth on the table or the chair arm and the head covered with a beautiful crochet filet pattern? To the maker, the doilies were also a work of beauty and elegant touch.

There were crocheted tables. Crocheted curtains, potholders, edges, pats, and table runners. Some people's favorite was luxurious bedspreads. That is not to mention the clothes made for their families by women of the past days.

All right, we agree that some of the 1970s touches were a little wild, and we are delighted that years and trends have long gone. No, we never wanted an orange and green toilet paper cover to match a crocheted toilet tank.

Allow us, however, to switch back to the thirties, quarters, and fifties. This was the time when a home was decorated and cared for with love and pride as a warm, safe haven. There was more time to create, and a woman always knew how to knit and crochet. Now don't misinterpret me, I don't think the woman today is a homemaker any less than before. But women had more time to build the home environment and the many personal comforts and special touches.

There's so much tradition and beauty to discover and share in the crochet past. We do not want the patterns to be forgotten with age. Some of the old patterns will be somewhat confusing due to their abbreviations. I hope that in those cases, this list will assist a little.

- ac--across
- Bl--Block
- bgr--beginning of rnd
- bt--between
- chlp--chain loop
- Ch--Chain
- Dc--Double Crochet
- D tr--Double Treble
- Dec--Decrease
- Dtr--Double Treble
- h d tr--half double treble
- h tr--half treble crochet
- H dc--Half Double Crochet
- hdtr--half double treble
- Hdc--Half Double Crochet
- Inc--Increase
- indl--inclusive
- Incl--Inclusive
- kcl--knot chain loop
- ltr--long treble
- o.m--open mesh
- O--Thread or Yarn Over
- pa--pineapple
- P--Picot
- pcl--picot chain loop
- pc--popcorn st
- pt--point
- prr--previous rnd
- r--ring

- rf--repeat from
- Rnd--Round
- s.m--solid mesh
- s st--Single Stitch (sc)
- Sc --Single Crochet
- sec--section
- scp--scallop
- Sh--shell
- sk--skip
- Sl st--Slip St
- Sp--Space
- slp--small loop
- Sts--Stitches
- St(s)--Stitches
- Tr tr--Triple Treble
- Tog--Together
- Tr--Treble
- x st--treble cross stitch
- Yo--Thread or Yarn Over

SIMPLIFIED SIX CROCHET STITCHES

Ch or Chain crochet- A chain stitch is the start of every project. The stitch line of the chain is your foundation. Tie the knot when you end the yarn about one inch. Leave a loop full enough to quickly pull the point of your crochet hook. Place your hook in the loop and tie your thread around the hook before you pull it through the loop. This is your first chain, and now you repeat the amount in the pattern. The chain stitch is the start of almost any pattern.

The slip stitch is used mainly to bind two pieces of crocheted work together. To form a circle, in the round pattern to crochet. Let's take a slip, insert your crochet hook from your hook into the first stitch on the other end of the row. Place your yarn over your crochet hook, and then pull it back through your crochet hook along with the yarn loop.

Single crochet or Sc - Insert the crochet hook to next stitch to form this thread. Wrap your yarn around the crochet once and stitch it through, two loops will be on your crochet hook now. Wrap the threads around the hook and pull the thread between the two loops. One crochet is made.

Half Double crochet or Hdc -Wrap the yarn around your crochet hook before you put it in the next stitch to make half-double crochet. Wrap the yarn again around the hook and then pull it in the thread. Three loops will be on your crochet ring. Run the yarn over the hook once and draw all three loops over the line. Half-two crochets are made.

Double Crochet or Dc - Make a double hook when you wrap the yarn over hook and do insert it into another stitch. When the hook is via the stitch, wrap yarn over hook and pull it through. You've got three loops left on your hook now. Yarn again over the hook and put it on your hook through the first two bows. There are currently two loops on the hook. Wrap the yarn around the hook again and drop the two loops on your thread. There's double crochet.

Triple crochet or Tr or Treble - Loop your yarn around your crochet hook twice, then put it in the next stitch for a triple crochet stitch. Wrap the thread around the hook and draw the stitch again. Four loops should be on your line. Wrap the yarn again over the hook and pull two loops through the front. Continue to wrap the yarn over the hook and pull it over two loops until a single loop is left on your crochet thread. Triple crochet is produced.

Now that you see all the abbreviations, you can figure out what every stitch is doing to the piece. There are a few more terms you must learn to make the right size, etc. These are scales, asterisks, parentheses:

ASTERISKS (*) are used to signify that the specified number of stitches or steps is to be repeated. Like * 1 FM, one sc, one sc from * through, you make one double crochet, one single crochet, one triple crochet up to the end of the line.

GAUGE means the number of stitches or rows in a given area. Every set of directions lists the gage obtained when the designer worked with the specified yarn and hooks and is the gage on which the guidelines are centered.

For more extensive size instructions, PARENTHESES) You can also indicate that the group of stitches you include must repeat the number of times shown.
Now select the right crochet hook to make the piece chosen. The first of the sequence reveals the needles or hooks as follows:
U.S. English Letter of Millimeter

1---0 2------B
2---1 2 1/2---D
3---1 1/2 3------F
4---2 3 1/2---G
5---2 1/2 4------H
6---3 4 1/2--- I
7---3 1/2 5------J
8---4 6------K

9---4 1|2
10---5
11---5 1|2
12---6
13---6 1/2
14---7

We will cover THREADS AND YARNS now, while we prefer to mix yarn with crochet knitting and the cotton thread, the yarn or thread may obviously be creating of any synthetic, fiber or natural. The synthetics are always machine washable and are particularly desirable in an items such as the baby clothing, that require regular washing.

The weight of the yarn is determined by the style of the item you make. At the start of a pattern, the type of thread to use and the colors of most pattern yarns are indicated. When the more exceptional hooks are used for a sensitive, soft impact, lighter weight cotton yarns or threads are usually needed. More massive hooks are used for a more rugged feel. Do not use other yarns if possible, as such instructions have been written for the specified yarn in order to determine the size of the garment. Follow always the guidance of your pattern and your crocheted piece is an object you can enjoy.

Crochet Important Tips

We all remember the saying the Practice is better. You will notice in crochet that this is really real, but it won't take too much practice to perfect your stitches. Enjoy your crochet, and follow these essential tips for good crocheting.

Tips

1: The first time you learn to crochet the whole process, you'll have to fasten the thread, yarn, and do it at the same time as trying to create various crochet stitches. But working at it, practicing the stitch does not take long before it feels normal. One good idea for the basic stitches is to start to make a lot of different Granny squares (or an enormous square) to use them to move the hook naturally and easily. You can even tie them together at the end and have a comfortable blanket.

2: The yarn is driven by your fingers as you crochet, which really generates your work stress and decides how strong your crochet is or not!

Looking at a crochet thread, you can see that it tapered inside as it reached the actual knot, and it had different thicknesses. The further away from the hook, it is thicker. So, if you let your loops go up the hook shaft, the loops are more significant, and the job is looser. Once the hook is closer, the loops are smaller, and the narrower the loops, the more the stitches are tightened. Therefore, when you operate along the hook shaft and not near the hook, bring the loops down to the hook and give the yarn another pulls to stretch the loops to lower the thickness.

Sometimes your stitches have to be tightened even more. To do so, just pull your crochet yarn at the end of the just-formed stitch again.

Crochet tension is especially important for clothing in most crochet projects. The scale of the finished garment determines stress. The thinner of the yarn and also the smaller of the hook you will crochet, the lower the end project will be and vice versa. So test your crochet tension against the pattern to make sure the finished item is correct. Alternatively, start crocheting when stress, such as a mat, chalk, or a Granny Square, is not so necessary.

3: Always take the time to prepare a practice swatch when creating projects where tension is vital. At the start of a project, this added time saves you time and heartbreak later. The practical samples are only practicing crochet bits using the hook and thread that the fabric is made of. (The practical swatch guidance is also provided in patterns where applicable.) Patterns inform you how many rows and stitches a certain length and width would suit.
Remember that you don't have to use the same yarn or hook as in crochet patterns. When your tension is too tight or too loose for the particular crochet pattern, your change will alter the finished project size. Cautiously, check for tension by crocheting a practice swatch to double-check dimensions if you use a different thickness yarn or a different size hook. This is important only when you make crochet clothing.

4: Relax and enjoy your crochet; your work will truly show. Do not hold your hook or yarn too close, or too loose. Look back at your stitches and make sure they all have the same size. Try to allow your crochet hook to move freely and tighten the yarn after each crochet stitch is finished.

5: Always hold your job. Your finger and thumb should hold your crochet just below where you stitch.

6: Always do it in a chain stitch with new yarn balls and make sure that it is at the end of a row, straight-line crocheting makes it easier to weave the yarn ends. Tip 6: This would also have more skilled completion.

7: It's not easy to crochet with fun hair because of its long eyelashes. This is not at all easy for beginners, because these eyelashes make it very difficult to see your crocheted stitches. If you can not see your stitches, it is tough work and can be very frustrating to place your hook correctly in the back and front of the stitches. So it's straightforward to go wrong.

By attaching another ball of yarn of a different kind (any kind without a pin) to the fun fur and crocheting each yarn simultaneously, you can clearly increase the stitches and make the job much easier to work with. This makes the thread and therefore works much thicker, so make sure that this always fits and adjusts hook sizes accurately if a garment is made.

AFGHAN CROCHET PATTERNS TIPS AND INFORMATION

A way of making an artwork out of several pieces of thread in yarn, in a particular aspect of sewing, crocheting is yet another kind of plan that allows a person to make something from a simple element.

This process allows you to produce a special kind of baby dress, hat, or any clothes you can use to make the fashion statement. Different elements can also be created by combining soft materials such as the yarn and the different basic "crochet stitches."

Afghan was used and reused again, and transmitted from baby to old, from a generation to another as remained fashionable and durable cloths after some years.

What's the reason for this? This is based on the manner in which the item was produced. This is because Afghans are made by remarkable crocheting methods. With the meticulous combination of various crochet stitches and the creator's careful handling to create good material, crochets of Afghan are indeed one of the best products this kind of leisure has ever produced.

Afghan history can be traced back to the time of "Afghan Oriental Rugs." Most people argue that famous teapots look like Afghan crochets. Therefore, most people since then have begun to associate this type of crochet with the oriental teapot. Even though it was not clear if the word "Afghan" was derived from standard rugs, the word only remained as the past grew.

Interestingly, people who try to know the basics of crocheting regard the creation of an Afghan as their first full-scale effort. The concept of Afghan crochet making is straightforward and easy. However, the critical component in the making of Afghan crochets is the use of simple crochet stitches and various Afghan crochet patterns.

The pattern is along with the simplicity of the piece. In fact, experts in crochet argue that, as with all sewing efforts, crocheting would not be easy to handle if no patterns were available as a guide.

After its inception, there have already been several different patterns of Afghan crochet created on the market. This is linked to the demands of the "crochet fanatics," who asked for more patterns to be used to produce results that are more diverse.

However, even though the organization today incorporates more modern Afghan patterns, the simplest and most fundamental crochet of Afghan patterns are still the best ones.

To learn more, here's a rundown of the most popular and most natural Afghan crochet patterns to use:

1. One can use a single crochet pattern to make a simple yet exquisite Afghan crochet. One good thing about this design is that it uses a pattern of stripes with different colors or a dense and continuous color.

With their solidity, a single crochet pattern is usually used for Afghans when they create a cover for a chair or a bed.

2. The Granny square is one of Afghanistan's most common crochet patterns. Based on its name, this Afghan crochet pattern requires the use of various types, including circles or squares. These shapes are individually crocheted and attached to different motifs and figures.

3. Chevron's crochet stripe pattern is beneficial for people who just learn crochet. It's an excellent way to learn the essentials of crochet while at the same time trying to create a masterpiece.

These are a few of the most Afghan crochet patterns that anyone would like to use. If patterns you use for Afghan crochet, be sure to note that the true beauty of the product is focused on why it was made.

MORE ESSENTIAL TIPS OF CROCHET

When you start crocheting and have mastered the simple stitches, there are still a few issues that hinder your work and ruin it. By following these crochet tips, you will ensure that your work is cleaner and even finished every time you crochet.

Not enough time for round jobs

Sometimes it does not seem as though there is enough room for the correct stitches in the center of the ring when operating in the circle. When you do not work over the previously worked stitches, do the following: If you have this problem:

- Enlarge your hook's last loop and remove your work's hook.
- Push the stitches together from the beginning of the round to create a gap at the end of the series.

- Attach your hook again, close the loop and start to crochet.

- Repeat this cycle until the round is done.

Accidental gaps or stretched stitches in your job

You will sometimes notice that you have some holes in your crochet that should not be there, or that some stitches seem to have expanded as it appears in the next section. The explanation is typically simple; in the previous row, you don't crochet into the right part of the stitch.

This will be corrected, so that after putting your hook in the stitch below, you have passed all stitch loops, unless the pattern tells you otherwise, as in looping hole patterns.

Split frames.

Do not just leave it if you notice a split stitch. This makes your work look very uneasy as it goes small sections of stitches across the pattern that are very apparent and detract from the right crochet pattern. The time it takes to correct these split stitches is rewarded by the smooth and sweet look of the work.

When you find a split point to remove your crochet hook, undo it all, and even the split thread, reinsert the crochet hook and re-start crocheting. It's worth the extra effort!

Finding it difficult to crochet in the base row.

Any crochet project's first line is always the hardest. It can be tough to crochet into a chain of points, mainly if you use thin yarn and a small hook!

If the first row you find difficult to crochet, try crocheting the row with a hook that is one size larger than that required for the pattern. It makes the base row of the chain a little looser and the stitches a little more full. This won't show the end result but will help you to insert your standard hook into your many chain stitches.

Starting to curl crocheting.

If you find that your work starts to curl after working the first few rows, it is because of your tension when you are working the straight-line technique. You crocheted the foundation line tighter than the rest of the pattern. You have two ways to solve this:

- Using a hook of one size larger than the hook used to crochet the pattern.

- Using the same anchor, but loosen your work (foundation row).

Difficult to see where to crochet.

This can be challenging to see exactly where you should crochet when you first learn to crochet, especially if you're using dark-colored yarn. So you can use light-colored yarn and threads when you first learn crochet, which makes stitches so much easier to see. Progress towards darker colors as your knowledge and trust grow.

Stitches losing.

Counting the stitches is one of the essential tips for good crocheting. This is also one of the most common problems to find that you have fewer stitches after crocheting a row than the pattern says or from which you have to continue if you do not follow a crochet pattern. The most common mistake is to lose stitches at the start and/or end of rows. This is because of the inability to operate in the first or last point of a sequence. So if you are in this place, check your beginnings and ends before you take a look at the body of the row itself!

Rectangular indoor or outdoor tapering

This question continues from above and is due to stitches that increase or decrease without knowing them! You will periodically count your stitches to ensure you have neither lost nor increased them unintentionally. The loss or the addition of stitches at the beginning or end of clothes is the most common mistake and should be checked before the row body is inspected.

Hopefully, some of the tips for your next crochet project would be useful. Only note these tips when you pick up your crochet hook will make your crocheting look more professional and clean.

CHAPTER THREE

Single Crochet for Beginners

This pattern teaches you how to crochet a simple crochet dishcloth ideal for beginners. The dresser pattern is easy to crochet to any size, making the pattern great for clothes, scarves, or whatever.

You will need a worsted weight of # 4 yarn to get started. You will obtain the details on the yarn labels. Used an H/8-5.00 mm hook for your crochet hook, but an I/9-5.50 mm works just as well for this yarn and pattern. It's just going to be a little bigger.

Make 21 chains to crochet the dishcloth.

Row 1: The Single crochet on the hook 's second thread. The missed chain is not a knot. Then single crochet through each row. Switch your life. Transform your life. (You 're going to make 20 stitches.)

Blocks 2-24: Chain 1. Then the work one single crochet through every thread. Turn after each row. switch after each row. (20 points in each row)

When you don't worry about the jagged edges, you can keep the fabric as it is and clean it off. Nonetheless, you can work around a single crochet stitch for an excellent smooth finish. Make chain 1 to do this. Then operate one single crochet equitably in each corner with three single crochet stitches. When you're around, you enter a slip stitch in the ring. You can now mount it and weave it in to protect it.

The above sequence can also be used to make a scarf or blanket. The only thing you want to change is the number of chains from which you continue.

You might need to start with fewer chains when making a scarf; around 15 would receive a right width. Then just repeat the second row until it's as long as you like.

What about a blanket, based on the size, you can start with 100 or 200 or more. A crocheted blanket would need just about a hundred, whereas a complete sheet would need to have a more significant range.

An even worse alternative is to change the size of your yarn and hook. Necessarily, you can choose whatever yarn and hook size, just ensure that your chains are calibrated to get the width you need. You can also add beautiful strips by changing the colors each row or each row.

HOW TO CROCHET USING EXTENDED SINGLE CROCHET

In this, you'll learn about extended single crochet and how you or your family and friends can whip up a nice crochet dishcloth. The crocheted blanket pattern is provided in one size, but in a single multiple of two, you can significantly impact that to any shape you desire.

An extended single hook is usually shortened as ESC. A crochet stitching is basically an extension of the single crochet and results in a beautiful textile. It's a little softer than single standard crochet, making it perfect if you want something with fashion and elegance.

To create the extended crochet single: Place the hook in the specified thread, yarn and pull up a loop, and yarn on and pull through a loop.

You'll need a worsted cotton yarn with an H/8-5.00 mm crochet hook to make that crochet dishcloth.

The size of this dishcloth is 7. by 7.25 inches finished.

To continue with, chain 22,

Row 1: (the Esc, chain 1) 2nd hook line, * skip next line, (ESC, chain 1) next chain; repeat * around. Row 1: (11 sc) flip.

Row 2: (the Esc, chain 1) in each of the first ESC and across. [11 dc]. Switch. Turn.

Rows 3-16: Row 2 is the same. Do not tighten, but continue with the border below.
Again for Edging, you can now continue to work from around dishcloth.

Round 1: Chain 1 and the single crochet work about 19 stitches on each side and three stitches on each corner uniformly. (88 points)

Round 2: chain 1 (ESC, ch 1) in the same stitch as a link, slip stitch on next thread, *(ESC, ch 1) in next thread, slip stitch in next stitch. Connect and loop at ends. Connect.

You could increase this size by increasing the starting chains in two or more instances. And this also means you can quickly make the bedroom or the sitting area with a baby blanket or a full-size blanket. If you make blankets, you can also turn to an acrylic yarn because it is cheaper.

You can also make an elegant scarf as there are fewer chains. It's also simple to crochet in circle, so it's perfect for legwarmers, bags, cowls, hats, or something.
This sequence would look fantastic when you turned colors up in every row or round. You are an artist, and there are infinite opportunities.

Study Crochet Stitches

Crochet is a process in which cloth with a thread or yarn and crochet is made. Crochet is similar to knitting as both methods involve drawing yarn loops from other loops. The only difference is that only one loop is used at a time, and instead of needles, a crochet hook is used. Crochet has existed for years, and studies over the years have created more and more designs. Crochet is also used to make shirts, blankets, scarves, home decorations, and even bikinis. In comparison to knitting, crochet is made only by hand.

Small CROCHETS

It is straightforward to understand, and there are other variations beyond the main methods. These stitches are built on a series of loops known as links. The stitches may be worked on their own or merged into designs. The fundamental crochet stitches are:

- Link-loop spring
- Twice the triple
- Treble. Treble.
- Half-double hook
- Stitch break
- Double Hook
- Single Hook
- Triple treble

TO Knit HOW

Products:

- Crochet hook
- Yarn of Crochet

Instructions:

- Hold the crochet hook between your index finger and thumb as if you catch a crayon.

- Next, make a chain of crochet. Create a slip-knot around the hook to do this. Wrap the yarn around the crochet and stretch it through the loop in the knot. The yarn is wound around the crochet.

- Draw another loop and repeat it until you've established multiple loops and are able to keep the yarn securely, i.e., not too tight or loose.
- You 're going to single crochet next. Keep the chain and insert the hook from the loop into the second chain.
- Bring the yarn across the hook, as when you made the chain, and draw it through the chain through which you inserted the string. Two loops must be on your line.

- Wrap yarn through hook and draw it to create single crochet using the two loops on the thread.

- To build the next thread, this time, insert the hook into the next chain in the chain line and repeat the appropriate instructions at #5 and #6.

- Continue to the end of the row where you are to form a chain to begin row 2. This chain means the turning link.

- Turn your job so that you face the line you have just completed. Place the hook under the two nearest top loops.

- Yarn across and pull the loop through to make the hook with two loops.

- Bring the yarn over the hook and pull back. Replicate to the end of the row and repeat until you can move on to various stitches.

Instructions to Make You a Pro Fast

Question crotchetier or knitters whether you should contemplate their specialty, and they'll likely expect it since craftsmanship is the most flexible and beautiful. Numerous individuals propose you are quicker, and others are chicer. Starter stitch is anything but difficult to learn, so it is simpler to utilize enormous snares so yarns. You will know for yourself whether you are on the whole correct to weave or stitch.

This is a profoundly flexible and standard procedure for making an assortment of style frill and home enrichments. You make a sensitive, clean texture by blending straightforward knit lines and lighter or heavier yarn; a thicker yarn makes a tough material. Beautiful finished and brought fastens up in sew are especially simple to make.

What you have to do is to sew a consistent yarn strand and a single catch. You start with a slip affix and continue making circles, confining a foundation way. Knit fastens are worked around the snare utilizing circles and wrapping yarn.

You could knit in line, keep your work level, or join fastens, ring, and workaround. You have a great deal of free examples on the web to begin you off. There's something on the web knit has for everybody. Pick something handy for you, with the goal that when you're done, you have some intrigue. Try not to begin with anything complex. Make certain to follow rules for the sort of example you are never helping to knit. A stitch eBook is ideal for that.

The Granny Square plan is one of the most realized knit structures. Such bright stitched squares or circles are joined to make afghans and coats. A Granny Wrap was a significant accomplishment in a Fall European couture assortment and was even included in an ongoing front of Vogue Magazine.

Weaving is a since quite a while ago settled sweater procedure due to its detail and shading designing and the delicate and solid texture made by the fastens. The two basic focuses sew and unadulterated can be worked alone or together, framing the base of many structures and different lines.

Two needles and a persistent yarn strand are required for sewing. You start by putting a slip hitch on one needle and "cast" the quantity of lines you requirement for the task. The base join are made utilizing the two needles, folding the string around one needle and drawing the wrapped yarn through circles on one needle. (That is the term for building the establishment line on one needle.)

Weaving needles-long, adaptable needles with a point at each end-are developing in prevalence as they maintain a strategic distance from creases and need to turn the sewing toward the finish of a line consistently. It is important to screen the development of your hands while taking care of the needles. You need a solid weave to make the completed item increasingly rich.

Wrapping, turning, and interlacing yarn offer unlimited opportunities for home and design. Make unbelievable silk tufts, turn a few strands of yarn in occasion wreaths, tear yarns to make your preferred outfit, or simply have a ton of fun wrap boxes. The alternatives are boundless, simple, and pleasant.

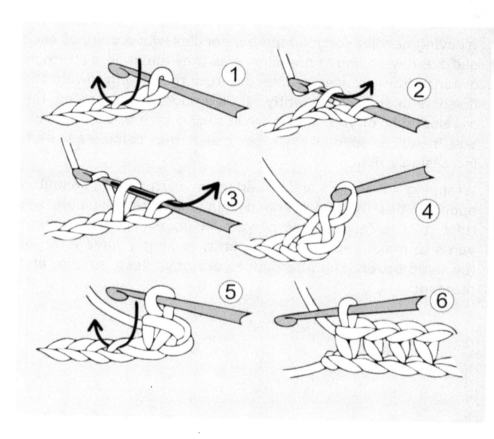

HOW TO DO BEADED CROCHET ROPE

All know small rounded-off glass beads. On our hand sacks and beautiful accessories, on clothes, on paintings, on jewelry, and everywhere, we will see them. There is no reason why crochets could not be used!

It will not be a good idea to be using these beads for our sofa covers, pillow covers, or even to decorate our hands and crochet hats? Such beads may bring to a daily pattern a new perspective on life.

I'm sure you'll love this way once you learn to make a beaded rope in crochet. No reason to despair, for here is your chance to learn and make your own crochet beaded. Try and understand that it is unethical for you to use silk or cotton thread in the cord because you will not go anywhere.

The reasons are that after some time, the massive design of these beads will work. They first make them loose, and then they let you cry out for your efforts. For beaded cords, polyester threads are recommended.

The more thing to know is that it is not easy to sew thread and put it on patterns because the thicknesses of the yarn make it difficult to move the beads. When you do a complicated design, it can ruin your job. Now it's time for me to begin how to crochet bread.

What to do are:
- You need a size ten polyester thread, crochet hook, size eight glass beads.

- Bring in the thread beads. Take another thread and fifteen positions. Now leave a chain to capsize and get the hook in the middle of half of the first half of the chain, to begin with, a single crochet stitch. Draw the last bead you have, add next to the strings and lock.

- Place the wool over the bead (yarn over the hook) and draw the circle. You have two hook loops, whereas the dot must be adjacent to the chain base.

- Similarly, create second wool; draw a loop that will result in a crochet stitch. Bead has only been worked on for the first yarn; the other thread is a traditional single crochet stitch.

- Replicate all fourteen (remember the first chain we skipped)

- Circular patterns can, therefore, be formed. In the complete circle, you would have to attach the first chain rope to the last with the help of a slip point.

- More rows are inserted according to preference or design requirements.

PUFF STITCH MAKING

A puff stitching is a beautiful medium crochet stitch that can be used in different patterns to produce textures on the crocheted fabric. Suitable for roses, afghans, shoes and wallets, scarves, hats, and other clothing items, as well as excellent home decoration, including pills, doilies, and pillows.

The texture of the puff stitch is noticeable on both sides, unlike other textured crochet stitches, such as the popcorn stitch. It is also suitable for scarves and other products where both parties are shown.

There are variants of this stitch, as with most other crochet stitches, and it is vital that each pattern is reviewed to recreate the identical pattern design.

To simplify it, the puff stitch is simply generated by drawing a number of loops on the crochet hook. The yarn is folded around the snare and inserted into the stitch, chain, or loop to pull the loops. The thread is rolled and drawn again. Each loop is sufficiently high to suit the previous stitches in the row.

The previous steps are repeated in the same stitch, chain or loop several more times until there are enough loops on the hook. Any time the steps are repeated, two more loops are attached to the ring, which means that the number of loops is inconsistent. Once the correct number of loops is on the hook, the yarn is wrapped, and all loops are drawn. The point is then fastened by a cord.

A puff stitching can indeed be made small enough to have been worked in a row or round in any stitch. However, it can contribute to further details with other stitches around the puff stitch, and spread between chains can contribute to an excellent latest design.

The puff stitch is, as mentioned, suitable for a wide range of crochet designs. The stitch will look like the shape of a flower petal depending on how many loops are made and how it is integrated into the pattern. It's thus a dominant stitch to create tiny flowers or Afghan flower squares.

Mostly, a yarn or crochet thread may be used to stitch the cloud. The only thing is that it uses a little more yarn than many of the other crochet points.

HOW TO MAKE CROCHET POPCORN STITCH?

Although it is quite straightforward to make a popcorn stitch, it's not really recommended for beginners or even for advanced beginners. It is implemented at the middle stage when the concepts of crocheting have been mastered already.

This stitch has several variations, but all have a similar effect. But to be on the safe side and to ensure that they look as intended, very often check the correct variation on the pattern.
The stitch consists of simple double stitches, which are pulled together to create a bump on one side of the fabric. The number of stitches can vary from pattern to pattern, but it is usually around four to five.

This stitch group is processed in a single stitch or chain. Therefore, the hook is removed from its loop, and the first double crochet in the group is inserted from the end. Then the dropped loop is picked up again and pulled through the first double crochet to close the popcorn stitch. This leads to the stitches appearing on the front of the tissue.

The popcorn stitch can also be closed to appear on the back of the fabric. To do this, we follow the same directions, except that the hook is inserted from the end of the first double crochet stitch. The dropped loop is then picked up from the front rather than from the back, and the extra points are then moved to the end. It is a helpful way of placing all popcorns in rows on one side.

If the popcorn stitch is the first stitch in a crochet row or in a round, the first popcorn stitch is called. The only difference at the beginning of the popcorn stitch is that three chains have been completed. These chains are usually the first double crochet in the group, meaning that the dropped loop is picked up and pulled through the third chain.

The starting popcorn stitch can be placed in the same way as a regular stitch on the front or back of the work.
Popcorn stitches look great in almost any thick or thin yarn. They are used in shoes, hot pads, footwear, and dishwashers. They also look beautiful in lactation, such as tablecloths, doilies, and other sophisticated decoration.

Crocheting And Knitting

Crocheting/knitting is among those tasks that seem a lot harder. You might ask a friend or family member who knits/crochets to show you how. If you don't know anybody, then you can take a lesson or join a student group in your local community college.

Crochet and knitting (also knitters and cricketers themselves) are without prejudice or prejudice, and there's something that is going to warm others up in hard times within a knitter or crocheter. Even if the artisan takes his own choice to the craft, only good will eventually come from it. Knit crochet stockinet is different from the knit stockinet hook stockinet. While crochet stockinet fabric can be made in many ways, it is unrealistic to expect that it will act as if it was knit.

Changes in size are then rendered by adding or subtracting stitch numbers from each model fabric. Add the towel towels to ordinary towels and give them a brand new look! This design gives you two different ways to add your sheet. Advanced crochet will make your beautiful pieces with fine yarn as an exquisite lace. One of the benefits for the beginner, however, is that it is straightforward to get going because the resources you would need at the start are natural and small.

The crochet pattern in rows is charted row by row. It starts with the foundation chain. There are many and varied patterns. From clothes created by combining several motifs to those produced in a single piece

Anyone sewing needs to knit better. Whatever project you are working on, you want it to look fabulous, as if you purchased it from a top designer. All want to leave their daytime jobs to have a full-time crochet design job. While some people can earn a living from design, they most often use it as a second income.

Understanding why you do certain things and why they work out increases trust and results in successful crocheting. Understanding this will help you to decide how your product will be placed on the market.

Everything in crochet is complicated by one of the simple stitches. You learn math, and you learn to add, multiply, subtract, and divide when you learn math. Anything that can be used and washed and creates a friendly, helpful fabric. I suggest working with cotton if you make a washcloth.

Actually, with double and triple crochet stitches, you can do a lot! By looking at most patterns, they are made of that (plus, of course, the single stitch), and it's the yarn that generally gives the interest.

All must be purchased and paid for. Even the air for which you breathe must be charged. With this lovely compilation of crochet and knit flowers, everything comes up roses. You can use these scraps with novelty yarns to furnish clothing, chains, bags, and belts, decorate home accessories or make a lovely bouquet as a rare showcase.

KNITTING 101

If some people talk of knitting, they picture little grandmothers who spend hours slowly, but no longer. Knitting is a great hobby which can bring pleasure and relaxation to everyone- without, mentioning lovely blankets, scarves, hats, clothes and more! You will learn to make homemade knits with just a little practice and patience for yourself and all the people you love. When you give a lovingly knit gift, some of you get into it and create a unique treasure of its own. Your time, talent, the vivid color of the yarn you choose, even your sentimental thoughts and feelings, all of which are part of your wonderful knitted gift.

The oldest known knitting examples were found in Egypt. At the final moment of the first millennium after AD, finely decorated cotton socks were discovered. Although experts think this was the origin of knitting, in Paris, France, in 1527, the first knitting trade association began. Knitting today is a common hobby and passion for people of all ages. Statistics from the Craft Yarn Council of America show that the number of female knitters aged between 25 and 35 has increased by 150 percent in the United States between 2002 and 2004 over two years. Today it is so popular that many groups and classes are now formed to share this entertainment and hobby with others.

Although some choose to join a party or class, other people tend to knit in their own privacy. There are few things to bear in mind before beginning a new knitting project. Find a cozy, comfortable chair or sofa for a long time, where you can feel relaxed to function. Always sure that the chair is well lit in the office. Another essential thing to note is to read any instructions or steps before beginning. Please note that it takes patience and practice to learn a new skill, such as knitting. But you should remember most of all, having fun when knitting. When you get stuck or frustrated, take a break with a short stroll, have a snack, or even a drink before returning to your current knitting project.

Most knitters start first with a cast-on stitch. Casting-on is the word to make the stitch base row on your needle. For beginners, intermediate and even experienced knitters, this type of stitch is recommended. However, have it in mind that there are many different casting methods. Some casting styles include the single-stitch, the double-stitched, the crochet bottom, the long-stitch, and the cast-on cord. Experts agree that knitting cast-on should be recommended as your first form since it is simpler and leaves your project with an extended edge. You may want to explore the other cast-on methods when you become a more accomplished knitter.

The next step in exploring knitting, once you have cut down, is the knit stitch that is also known as the garter stitch. Merely speaking, knitting is the art of creating a textile by locking yarn loops using two basic ways to create these loops. The first way is to 'stitch' your needles through the bottom of a circuit and pull a new circuit and through the primary circuit. The other method is called 'purling' or removing the needles from the top of a loop and pushing a new loop up from the first thread.

Gauge is another significant knitting element. Gauge refers to a number of rows and stitches a cutter produces with a specific type of yarn and needles or crochet per inch. Gauge varies significantly from person to person, so it is essential to make sure your particular pattern is measured. Basically, the size of your finished piece determines. Therefore, if you don't get the right size, the garment won't get the right size. When you knit with a thick yarn, you can make bigger stitches and have very few rows per inch. You will create smaller stitches and have more stitching and rows per inch when you knit with more beautiful yarn. To determine an accurate swatch, cast or chain sufficient stitches to about four" and work in a 4" pattern. Take your stitches off the needle and place a tape measure on your work without extending the fabric and gently pin where the tape reads one inch.

You should also be aware of the various varieties and types of handles to knit with when addressing gauge. Classic circular needles with today's knitters are a standard option. The double-pointed needle is another common alternative. And needles like the straight needles are perfect for knitting lace. The tips on these needles are tapered so that the digging into a stitch is easier. Growing needle-type has various advantages and should be tested according to what you want and what type of project you are working on.

After learning the basics of knitting, you can start thinking about and focusing on the ribbing. Ribbing is a border commonly used to knit on the cuffs of those cozy hats, sweaters, and scarves. It is used because a stretchy fabric is produced and made with a combination of the knit stitches and purl stitches we previously touched upon. Ribbing with any number of stitches is possible, but the most common is two or three.

There are a number of critical steps and points along the way to learn the ability to knit. What is so beautiful about knitting is the range of options available. You and only you can create many different colors, types of yarn, needle, stitch, pattern, and looks-making your knitting project a perfect artwork, that can never be reproduced.

CHAPTER FOUR

Care for Knitted Fabrics

For short, pilling

Pilling is a word you may have heard, and it is a disease you may have experienced. But do you even know what pilling means? Pills are, to a greater or lesser degree, accidental and unwanted small clumps or yarn balls on the surfaces of almost all knitted fabrics. Their presence marks the appearance of knitted clothes, giving them a tired, worn outlook. So, what are you willing to do with pilling? You can begin by understanding its four basics:

I) The pilling causes; II) Where it is possible that pilling would occur; III) Pilling can be reduced in ways; and iv. When you can take pills safely.

What is triggering pilling?

Abrasion or friction may cause the yarn to be separated by regular use and cleaning of the knitted cloth. Short fibers are separated and loosened from longer fibers in a twisted yarn. The loose last of these short fibers then clump into tiny balls. Such pills are what we know as pills and what we call pilling is their presence in knitted clothing. Small bits of lint are also taken in clumps, making the pills even stronger.

Where is the pilling in a knitted garment likely?

As abrasion is catalytic to pilling, the areas with the enormous friction of your knitted garments are most likely to form pills. The underarm area comprises the sweaters, coats, vests and clothing; sleeves' undersides; the socks' heels; and shorts and slippers' inner thigh area.

When you wear knitted surfaces and sit down on a desk all day, irresistible pills can even grow in areas that frequently come into contact with your office or equipment, which include the long-sleeve or wrist area that rubbed against the edge of a computer keyboard; the elbow area of a shirt, if you, like many people, prefer to rest on your desk while talking on the phone and the front trunk of a top which rushes routinely against the edge of a desk or another work surface.

Some of these areas are so famous for their pilling and premature wear that they can be reinforced. Examples involve sweaters made with suede patches on the elbows from the beginning. Leather replaces knitted textiles in jodhpurs, pants worn while conducting equestrian activities, inside the calves, knees, and sometimes a panel in the rum area. Socks are often made from a mixture of animal and non-animal fibers that give the finished product stability.

Why will pilling be minimized?

If you knit your own fabric on garments that have areas subject to abrasion, you want to select your yarn carefully. Start by inspecting your yarn, mainly if it is a yarn for which you did not work in the past, and reading the label of the factory. Unless the ball strip indicates to wash or dry the fabric, you may presume the yarn is fragile and can pill more quickly than a more durable thread does. The same applies to an item of purchased clothing with identical washing instructions on the care tag.

Next, treat a small yarn length. Roll a strand between your fingers to decide how quickly the strand breaks into component strands. The short animal fibers are more comfortable to free if the strand is readily separated. The higher the number of the filament and the tighter the yarn twists, the less likely it is that the pilling will be necessary. In comparison, loosely twisted yarns are more natural to pill when treated by your fingers.

You don't need to stay away from delicate yarns, and you might want to know how best to use them. Suggest reinforcing responsive parts of the garments by working in a color-coordinated nylon thread. You could knit a double strand to increase your delicate yarn by knitting it together with a more durable strand of yarn. And maybe you should save the most delicate yarns for less stressful garments.

Avoid washing machines wherever possible. The easiest way to launder is to wash the knitted garments by your hand, even though the manufacturer of yarn or garments suggests that the drying or washing process is appropriate. Be careful to pinch the cloth while washing hands, not to curl it, wring it, or rub it. Know, abrasion induces pilling, so you don't want to place an unnecessary pressure or tension on your knitted garment while washing your hands.

Dry cleaning is also an alternative to hand washing, although a more costly one. Until cleaning clothing dry, please check for contraindications on the ball band or the clothing tag. If you leave your robe in the hands of a dry cleaner, take the time to talk to the cleaner about the knitted robe, the types of fabrics from which it is made, and any specific manufacturer's cleaning notes.

If you do washing machines, turn the garment inside out and wash it in a gentle process using a post of equally delicate clothing with a low propensity to wash. If the water level is set to a large load, but only a medium weight can be removed, your knitted clothing can move freely during agitation. With more space in the machine and more water around the garment, it will be less frictional and, therefore, less likely to pill. Manufactured softeners tend to decrease static attachment. Adding a liquid softener to the wash cycle would not only soften your knitted clothes but also reduce the appeal of lint. Any pill that develops will be less visible than if it is mixed with hair or bits of lint from other washing products.

How can you remove pills safely?

You may use many devices to extract pills from your knitted fabrics, and they all share some general instructions for their use and the preparation of the garments. Start by placing the garment on a clean, flat surface. Arrange the clothing where possible so that only a single layer of the fabric falls on the area of operation. To remove the pills, use one of the following tools. In your job, you may want to take time, use a gentle touch, and keep the fabric tightly in the area you are de-piling. If you know how a tool operates on a particular material, it is best to check a small, unfamiliar territory such as a sweater 's axis. Function only in one direction (e.g., from top to bottom, but not back and forth). However, if you strip pills with a shaver, using quick circular motions. Regardless of the device you use, make sure your area of work is illuminated, and you have a clear vision when you're working on the fabric.

Tools for particular purposes:

These gadgets are designed specifically for removing pills. They are available in most sewing and craft stores and are generally healthy if used according to their instructions and guidelines.

- Shirt raspberries.

- depilatory pebs (very fine dented tissue pebs).

- Sweater stones (light-grade stones)

- Sweater stones.

Safe multifunctional tools:

There are some other tools that, while not explicitly created for removal, nevertheless remove pills effectively. You are usually safe to use on your knitted fabrics when you apply the above guidelines carefully and correctly.

- Industrial sandpaper fine (150-180 or higher).

- Velcro (the "hooks" side).

Don't forget to check on a small spot, operate just in one direction, and keep a light touch.

Riskier multi-purpose tools:

A few other devices may be used to separate pills from knitted fabrics. However, these devices are more likely to cut or otherwise damage the underlying material and should be used with care. Again, it is essential that you follow the guidelines above, when using one of these (or any of) the tools for pill removal.

- Racers for disposable protection.

- scissors.

Be very vigilant when cutting knitted strings, sticks, crocheted tops, borders, buttons/buttonholes, and other stitches so as not to cut the threads. If you lack a steady hand, or feel uncomfortable with the tablets, ask your nearest dry cleaner. If you order various filters, you will provide the pills as a service; be prepared to pay for this service, of course.

Your knitted fabrics will remain fresh and last long enough to become a "treasured friend" through a little common sense and consistent care.

Equipment Is Needed To Learn Knitting Easy

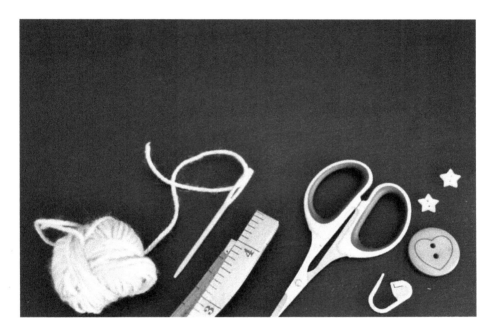

Knitting requires very little equipment for a garment, but it must be the best if you are to achieve maximum enjoyment and relaxation – although the excellent equipment alone does not produce perfect work automatically. For example, when the knitting needles are too weighty, too rigid or too folding, or if the needle has steep points that break the yarn or sharp points that hurt the fingers, knitting is a challenge, and this is reflected in the finished garment. Due to all the factors listed in the example, precise knitting needles should be obtained.

The specific needles are designed to slip through the stitches without splitting the thread, have the right balance, are light weighted and sufficiently durable to allow long working times without straining the hands and shoulders.

There are currently on the market a variety of decent knitting needles, some of which are:

• Silvalum (a particularly unique aluminum alloy with a permanently smooth finish which does not soil light-colored yarn and has a strong needle.

• Lucite is more versatile (plastic-like)

• Tonewood is indeed a beautifully made hardwood. However, it is generally only available in bigger sizes with needles (for ribbons, or very bulky yarns).

Knitting pins are made in single, double, or circular forms. The single-point crochet needles are often referred to as straight needles and are used for all knitting. On certain knitted pieces with seams that would hinder appearance and health, double-down needles (stock needles), are often recommended, including neckline finishes and many other purposes.

For several different types of work, circular knitting needles are used. They can be used for sleeves, ribbing the neck, and small apparel, sometimes for skirts, sweaters, coats, and dresses.

Strange as this sounds, whether or not you crochet, without a few crochet hooks, knitting equipment is not complete. Such hooks are required to finish a knitted garment and to collect "missing" stitches.

The following knitting aids are not mandatory but are intended to encourage the completion of a few small tasks that are needed to operate, complete, and add to the appropriate fit.

- Yarn pin-to sew the knitted and wool holding seams

- Knit Count-you can easily hold a number of rows when you twist the tiny dials

- Stitch makers-to securely hold the stitches if not in use. They are available in thin, medium, and large aluminum and plastic materials. Midget stitch holders are also suitable for carrying a minimal number of stitches.

- Cable stitching creator-the The curve tightly binds the stitches and enables cable stitching. In all instances, use the holder when instructions call for a new needle. The size of the knitting needle is appropriate for all types of yarn, regardless of the thickness.

- Bobbins for wool-spinning colorful and argyle socks. This yarn bobbin allows the yarn to relax smoothly and evenly; activate the thread as desired. This knitting aid avoids knots and tangles and holds a decent amount of yarn.

- Ring markers – to slide on the needle to mark the job for increases or decreases, etc. Valuable when making skirts or sweaters where it is challenging to count stitches.

- Knit Chek-built for more straightforward and more precise tests of the stitch and row size. You can not overemphasize the value of testing your scale.

- Tape count.

- Blades/Scissors.

- Clear 6-inch law.

- Catchy fingernails file and emery plate.

- Tapestry needles with a flashpoint.

- Pencil and journal.

- Small transparent case for quick access to all missing products.

Some of the above items needed for the home knitter are available to you in your own home; you have to buy some.

Only a few tips on gear before going shopping (if you haven't done that) if your equipment is old, keep a large, covered bottle of stainless needles and hoods out of rust, with a small piece of camphor wrapped in cloth (available from any Watkins dealer).

Wooden needles that grow rough and enticing spots can be healed by plunging a lightly damp cloth into a fine-grained kitchen cleanser, which can be used to smooth the needle. Allow the syringe to dry thoroughly, then rub with a raw cloth and polish with a dick fold of waxed paper all the dry cleaner.

If your fingers get sore with rough or knotty yarn, cut your finger off an old child's glove and slip the offended finger- fantastic how this works!

Pay attention always for tips everywhere you go – watch them and find them somewhere. You never know if these tips and/or hints are useful.

Knit some clothes at home and, if so, what's your most useful idea for the first domestic knitter?

Know The Important Things Before Knit

Have you ever enjoyed yarn texture in your palm, or wondered how your favorite sweater made this fascinating color pattern? Then you'll definitely enjoy learning the knitting craft. Knitting is one of the ways to create fabric weaving and crochet: yarn or thread. Everything's about imagination.

The initial knitting measure.

In comparison to woven cloth, and knitted fabric that consists entirely of parallel horizontal yarn courses. The courses are connected by loops interlocking, that a shorter loop is extended around a sequence of yarn. Knitting can be taken out by hand or by computer, described below. What makes knitting even more fun is that it's easy to learn this craft.

In practice, hand knitting is typically started by forming a base collection of twisted yarn loops on the needle. This is known as Put On. A second needle is then used to touch a bunch of yarn through each loop in a row to pull a length back through the loop. This is a new level. Work may be carried out round (circular knitting) or in rows. Machines that use a different mechanical device to achieve substantially the same results can also be knitted.

Two basic types of knitting are available, English and Continental. The difference is the way you keep the yarn; the yarn is held in the right hand in the English method. The thread is kept in the left hand during continental knitting. Any approach should be able to master regardless of your natural hand preferences because the essence of knitting is ambidextrous basically.

The two basic stitches are plain or knit and pure or incorrect. Such two nominal stitches are, however, the opposite and the reverse side of the same thread. The combinations and variations of these two stitches establish all possible stitch patterns for knitting. In general, a knit stitch emerges from the insertion of the needle from a left-to-right perspective on the front of the loop to create a new loop, whereas a straight stitch is formed by the addition of the needle from a right-to-left perspective on the front of the loop.

A knitting element begins with the casting process, which includes the initial development of the stitches on the needle. The first step in knitting is to throw these stitches into the first row of stitches and into the jungles of your work, usually the edge or edge.

Different cast methods are used for different effects; one can be lace-stretched, while another can have a decorative edge. A temporary cast is used when the knitting starts from the cast in both directions.

A knitted piece may contain single stitches or a variety of colors and textured patterns. The number of active points is the same as when cast, without adding stitches-an increase or removal-to shape the object.

Knit patterns (Towards Online Income): Many people sit at home and publish significant knitting dummies from home. Over the years, many knitting patterns have been compiled and updated. By selling or distributing the modes on the net, they make a high income. If you've done enough, you can even earn some online money.

Many designs can be made in different combinations of knit and simple stitches. If only knitting or purling is used in line, the result is called a garter stitch.

The alternate rows of knits and purls result in the stockings stitch, also known as jersey stitch or storage stitch, used most commonly in commercial clothing, including T-shirts. Different stitch combinations may be used to shape ribbons, cables, or other textures.

The remaining live stitches will be cast off until the knitted piece is completed. Attach or tie the stitches over each other so that they can be separated without unrolling the object from the needle. Although the mechanics differ from casting, a similar variety of methods and choices are required. The Simple Bind-off and the Suspended Bind-off are the most flexible methods.

Knitted garments are most often made in pieces, where individual parts of the clothing are separately knitted and sewn together until all parts are finished. Seamless knitting is also possible where a whole fabric is knit as a single piece. Smaller things like socks and hats are usually knit on double point needles in one piece.

Knitting is easy to understand nowadays, as there are many knitting blogs and numerous books for beginners on the market, where step-by-step instructions can be found. These guidelines are so easy to follow that they are not difficult even for children. Show your imagination, take your knitting instruments, and learn to knit now!

MATERIALS AND CROCHET INSTRUCTIONS

Some people asked how to interpret the directions for Crochet. The following information may be helpful.

In addition, crochet instructions are not so easy to follow and read until you are aware of the pattern and significance of each abbreviated symbol.

Remember to check the dotting and pause every time you see intervals or commas in the instruction. The fundamental element in the study and teaching of crochet patterns is to understand the writing style, including crochet abbreviations. However, the symbols and abbreviations are not relevant to know instantly because if required, you can still refer to your list.

It can be very convenient to have someone by your side, reading the instructions clearly to you. While memorizing abbreviations is not essential, knowing them is vital so that you know what to do is necessary.

Instructions usually use parentheses) (and asterisks (*) to indicate repetition patterns.

For instance, when the pattern tells you to "repeat from *," you need to look back and look at the row instructions that you are currently working on to find the asterisk (*). Crochet the direction immediately after this asterisk (*).

Sometimes, some patterns ask to "repeat from *" not only once, but more. If this is the direction, you will go back and find your asterisk (*) and then obey the guidelines on how much the pattern needs to be crocheted.

Generally, there is only one asterisk (*) in a row, and the "repeats" carry you to the end of the row so that no additional instructions are needed to finish the repetitions.

Some patterns use a "single asterisk" at the beginning and at the end of the "repeat." And when you hit the successor "single asterisk" (*), you are conscious that this is the place where this "repeat" will end.

In some cases, patterns use "single asterisk" (*) and "double-asterisk (* *), where typically the" double asterisk "is used to indicate where you will finish the repeat; for example, patterns tell you to" repeat from * to * *, "search again in circular directions to find the asterisk (*).

Directions usually state "work even" that you will work on the same stitch and not decrease or raise stitches.

Here are things to remember while looking at a pattern for crochet:

- Crochet patterns and instructions usually work in circles and rows. Each crochet pattern explains what you're doing or working in circles, rows, or both of them.

- Nearly all crochet patterns, techniques, and directions usually rate according to difficulty level such as advanced, dull, intermediate, or beginner. Pick a pattern with a difficulty level that suits your skills, to avoid disappointment as you attempt to finish an advanced design.

- It's indispensable to count your work stitches, so you will be able to calculate how many stitches are needed in each round or row as required by the pattern.

- Test the gauge at any time. To do so, crochet a sample about 4 X 4 inches in the pattern, so your hook instructions use. If the measure is more considerable than the one indicated by the pattern, use a bigger hook. If it turns out the gauge is more significant, try to use the hook even larger.

- Registering for a crochet lesson can be very helpful when you start learning crochet. Never be disappointed when you get started if every pattern and its abbreviations cannot be understood. The reading and comprehension of crochet patterns require continuous practice.

Start with simple projects like the dishcloth, scarf, and potholders, or any quick and tiny design where you believe you can understand the directions. The satisfaction of creating your own art can encourage you to create various patterns at different levels for every finished project or piece.

Knowing enough about the interpretation of Crochet instructions helps to reduce the apprehensive aspect. You will have nothing to think about if you apply what you know about the crochet instructions.

CHAPTER FIVE

Advanced Stitches

You would quickly be bored with what you already know if you were a correct craft individual. In this case, as a crocheter, you can either try new stuff with your simple stitches or learn advanced stitches. Let's think about up-to-date stitches today.

One thing you must know about advanced points is that they are made only from the essential points. It is just that a particular piece or modification of basic stitches produces a specific shape like an Afghan stitch that is used as a stitch in turn. Simply put, an advanced stitch is made of thick of one or more fundamental stitches.

The clarification above takes us to another significant point. In other words, don't be afraid or too afraid of advanced stitches. Only refer to and follow the directions before you can do them smoothly.

Often it appears to be happening that you understand what to do but did not know the catchy title you gave. Follow the information double and proceed to work on the project. It's a hobby, something you do to relax. Be careful not to beat yourself to make it right.

Having recommended relaxing when studying advanced stitches, you need to realize that a detailed understanding of the basics and methods such as slip stitching, fixation, and joining is important as well. This fundamental understanding is the move to the next point. Intermediate and intermediate crocheters may use basic stitches. Beginners will wait to learn the fundamentals before going on.

There is, therefore, a world beyond the simple chain, sc, the slip stitch, dc, and triple and connection. Some are referred to as double triple (DTR), crochet cable, filet crochet, hairpin lace, tulip, and Afghan stitch.

Advanced Beginner Crochet Skill

The second level of ability is the advanced level of beginners, also known as pure. This level helps you master all the fundamental points, and often requires you to combine them in short pattern sequences. If the basics have been mastered, the pattern sequences are standard.

The triple and double triple stitches are some of the harder stitches introduced at this level. At this point, you can also see further rises and decreases. At the end of a row or in the center of a row or around, the increases or decreases will decrease.

The best thing about this is that stitch abbreviations and other pattern details don't seem so overwhelming anymore. Your new confidence in your crochet ability and in following the written instructions will help you relax a little more.

Apart from reading crochet patterns, this is the stage where you can gain more confidence by reading crochet diagrams. The majority of models are generally written down, but a few even send you a symbolic map. While I prefer the written pattern, the picture is almost more comfortable to read because it helps you to look at the stitch pattern.

The pure level of ability is still considered to be a beginner level, so you still have to pay careful attention to the pattern and to your crochet. Ultimately, this will slow you down, and perhaps you may want to crochet a little faster. You will just figure out a pace that you have made a mistake somewhere. One common mistake is that the points are much looser, which then distorts the shape of the fabric. Therefore, patience and crochet at a comfortable and consistent speed are best practiced in order to make a regular fabric.

The best way to stay at this level is to master all the basic crochet stitches. The next level lets you use the basic stitches to create elegant combinations of stitches and lacy designs. Before you're ready, it can be tempting to jump to the next crochet level, but knowing the basics will make it a lot easier.

Basics of The Crocheting Animals

The way crochet creatures are made can seem incredibly daunting. They look really complicated and convoluted. There are endless possibilities for creating different animal species! It seems very unlikely that a whale, a dog, a snake, or even a lion will produce the same method. Fortunately, the procedure exists is simple and has crazy ways of using.

Once you figure out how to make these affectionate, soft dolls, you should be very used to single crocheting. It certainly isn't too complicated.

Details through solitary crochet guidance:

- Complete a small yarn section with a slip knot. Some people's favorite way to make a slip knot is to build a two-finger loop. Instead, they work to pull the yarn loop into the initial loop with their other hand. Secure knot slip every time!

- Stitch chain four times. The chain consists of placing the yarn over the crochet earth and pulling the thread back through the slip knot. It's pretty simple as soon as you're used to it enough.

- Insert the hook straight into the first stitch at the last stitch to build the loop. It is the beginning of one crochet thread. Yarn over and pull through the first stitch. You are going to see two crook loops. Yarn over the first loop drop. Yarn over again and pull the second thread. Your first single crochet stitch has been completed!

Follow the simple steps above and follow them if you intend to make crochet animals. If you want something romantic and cuddly, or you want to give friends and the individual family presents, that is what you want!

The best approach to ensure trained, shapely crochet animals is to ensure that you can firmly join your own person crochet. When sewing, the joints should not be loosened too much as they are filled in the stitches. This creates an incomplete feel. Mind your unique crochet stitch!

You may wonder how every single crochet animal is created. Okay, the most widely used cuddly creatures are designed in the Amigurumi style. Here is the value of the counter and stitch marker! It is essential to keep track of the stitch and row as a way to ensure that the plump doll is modeled correctly. Tasty crochet, and enjoy it!

Long Scarf Crochet

There are numerous scarves on the planet. Some are beautiful and set aside a ton of effort to make. There are essential scarves that are helpful and snappy. This is the best way to knit a long scarf. This scarf can be worn by anybody. It is unisex. It is anything but difficult to make. It just includes making a chain and utilizing single sew fastens. When the first example is comprehended, the scarf can be made up to one wants. Ensure you realize how to make a chain and single knit before perusing this area.

The initial step to making this scarf is to have the correct apparatuses. Every one of the needs of the one is a size J knit snare, a yarn needle, and scissors to cut yarn. A tape estimated might be utilized if an exact length is wanted. For whatever period of time that the scarf is in any event two feet or twenty-four inches in length, it will be sufficiently long. Accurate estimation isn't required. It is up to the one creating the scarf to decide whether it is long enough.

When the instruments have been assembled, get the yarn wanted for the scarf. It is ideal to utilize a four handle yarn or Red Heart brand yarn. It is perfect to have a yarn that won't be excessively bothersome around the neck, yet will keep the one wearing the scarf warm. Any shading might be utilized.

Make a slip hitch in the yarn. At that point, utilize the knit snare to make the chain twelve or fourteen. This means by which enormous the scarf will be over. When chain is creating, single sew into each circle or fasten in the chain. Do this over the column.

When the fastens, have been made in the chain, chain one, and turn your work. Single sew into each attach over the column. When that line is finished, chain one and turn your work once more. A single line in each joins until the finish of the column. Chain one and turn your work. Rehash this example until the scarf is the ideal length. Ensure it is sufficiently long to wrap freely around the individual wearing the scarf's neck. Ensure it will hang pleasantly at the perfect height after it has been folded over the neck. Two feet or twenty-four inches is a decent, essential gauge of to what extent the scarf should be; however, it doesn't need to be that exact length.

Choosing Best Designer Handbag

It can be of the doubt to try to pick the right bag from the many luxury designer handbag choices on the market today.

It is no surprise that there are so many concerns about actual designer handbags, bags, and even bags for their appropriate use. Believe it or not, one of the topics most commonly debated is which designer handbag to purchase for a work interview.

One key point here is that first, then style, purpose comes first when it comes to engaging in a work interview or even business lunch. A practical handbag can easily contain essential documents such as your reference letters, portfolio or copy, and also the business cards without damaging them. Your designer's bag will reflect your distinctive sense of style throughout. Depending on personal choice, many women all together have a luxury designer handbag and hold a case.

Points to consider for a big work interview when selecting an authentic designer handbag are:

- Choose a versatile bag that includes many inner pockets that can store your most valuable items, such as designs, business cards, cell phones, and keys. In this way, you must not spill out all of the contents of your bag or rummage your hand through your bag to locate a particular object. The worst thing to do is just look disorganized because you don't know where anything is.

- Your luxury designer bag should be of a reasonable size so that you can hold your resume without folding it inside your pocket.

- A handbag with a sort of zipper, magnetic appendage, or Velcro eliminates the chance that during your interview, the contents of your bag will unintentionally fall out.

- Make sure that the color of your designer bag suits your outfit so that your interviewer can look presentable during his / her work application.

- If you attend an interview, you do not want to look too relaxed to try and avoid cotton or nylon handbags. A black or brown leather handbag will be the perfect option.

- No matter how chic your authentic designer's handbag is, it will not pass a precise examination if you have dumb blockages or stains on the outside of your bags. Keep it clean!

Anything to consider while looking for a trendy handbag for the designer:

If you wonder, the best place to see the latest and most popular evening handbags is by celebrities at significant award ceremonies or inauguration events for film and business enterprises. The best designs of the evening handbags, from fashionable clutches to elegant drawstring bags, are easily identified.

The specific luxury design of a handbag that you choose should make enough room for your money, lipstick, ID, and keys. You will need a slightly larger bag if you need your phone or digital camera. In addition, your evening handbag will add to your evening outfit. The rule of thumb is just that you can select a smaller bag with a black or a black trimming if your dress is black color. Another option is to use a bright color such as silver, red, or gold to highlight your entire outfit. The advice here is to find your evening bag as an extra accessory, as opposed to a requirement, like a necklace. Authentic designer evening handbags are offered in several styles that include crochet, silk, browsed, lace, satin, beaded, sequins, velvet, and bagpiping styles that suit every kind of outfit. With a thorough search, you will undoubtedly find the perfect match for your evening.

Stuff to remember when looking for a decent designer's travel handbag:

The number one thing to remember is health when shopping for a travel bag. This applies not only to the safety of the people with whom you travel but also to the security of your passport, travel papers, personal belongings, and currency.

Your most valued travel items, such as passport, credit cards, hotel keys, passenger checks, and other travel ID format, should be included as a travel designer handbag. A travel handbag with reliable, stable straps, internal storage, and magnetic or zip closures should be built. A variety of holidaymakers also bring a money pocket concealed under their clothes to discourage even more theft men.

Tips to spot real handbags before you buy them:

In major metropolitan cities like New York, Madrid, Paris, London, Los Angeles, or Toronto, it seems to be easy to find an authentic handbag, but it looks complicated. The unregulated selling of fake bags is, sadly, easy for street vendors and flea merchants who don't really care who they are to make fast cash. If you've purchased a designer brand name handbag from a street vendor in any of these cities, it's probably not a first. The exact location of the sale will be the first red flag to spot an authentic designer handbag. Any small tips on detecting fake goods:

- Take a look at the concept very carefully. You can know that it isn't just right when you look at it. If you think about it, the high-end designer manufactures high-quality handbags to typically detect imitations of low quality by looking at them. Check your inner stitching and smell the material or feel it. A genuine designer's handbag is almost perfect. The bag's colors are bright, and the internal lining and stitching are free from noticeable defects. In addition, a designer brand emblem etched or printed should be displayed somewhere on or inside the handbag.

- Request identification proof such as receipts or serial numbers. Authenticity cards are often followed by the most costly designer handbags. The authenticity card displays the company brand logo and usually includes some kind of serial number or a magnetic strip that is registered for the actual designer. Before you decide to buy this important stuff, make sure you see it.

- Typically, if the price is too reasonable to be accurate, if a brand name handbag were cheap, every person would own one on the street.

The option of an authentic designer's handbag is not rocket science, but critical questions have to be taken into account before you purchase one. Now that you know well how to choose the right handbags for your ever-growing outer garment, buy one. Please note that real designer handbags are available for all forms of real-life situations.

Security when shopping for a travel bag is the number one factor to consider. This applies not only to the safety of the people with whom you travel but also to the security of your passport, travel papers, personal belongings, and currency. Your most valued travel items, such as passport, credit cards, hotel keys, passenger checks, and other travel ID format, should be included as a travel designer handbag. A travel handbag with reliable, stable straps, internal storage, and magnetic or zip closures should be built. A variety of holidaymakers also bring a money pocket concealed under their clothes to discourage even more theft men.

The Filet Crochet

Filet crochet is a collection of crocheted mesh stitches that are crocheted in a particular sequence to form a distinct pattern or image. It's easy and fun to do, and super fast and finished effects can be excellent.

You may generate the image or pattern by following a pattern chart using a straight line technique or a mixture of either empty or filled mesh squares in a circle. We will only deal with this crochet article with the straight-line method.

The mesh stitches are composed of a triple and chain stitch combination.

Those are all the stitches you need to learn, except slip stitch, to make your own filet crochet parts.

Friction isn't so necessary when you crochet filet. The biggest thing is that the stitches are straight. If your tension is very wrong, rectangular mesh stitches, instead, typically do not affect the finished product or the pattern. If you want to make sure the mesh stitches are square, use the same size hook and thread to crochet a realistic swatch, you are going to use for the project you are doing. Then seek a different size hook if the mesh stitches are not square in shape.

The main thing is that the mesh stitches are all the same size and shape so that the filet pattern or image you want can be viewed easily.

In the creation of filet crochet, there are not many crochet stitches, and these are only the simple crochet stitches; chain stitch, slippery stitch, and triple seed. You will see other stitches, all composed of simple crochet stitches, to give filet crochet a slightly different appearance.

Typically, the filet crochet works with crochet cotton or thread. There's nothing you can avoid using some kind of yarn, however. Crochet cotton is available in various thicknesses, most commonly found in sizes twenty or thirty.

The size of the square mesh and hence the size of the finished component vary with various thicknesses of thread or different types of yarn. Please use the appropriate crochet hook size for your ribbon or yarn. Check the mark if in any doubt.
In order to measure the finished size of a product, crochet a practice swatch using the same crochet hook size and yarn/thread as the object. Then weigh five squares and then five rows down. See how many rows you'll crochet and see how many rows you have, name this number Z.

Divide Z by five and then multiply it for the rows with your calculation. That's how long the work will be done. Now look at your pattern again and see how many squares it has in a row, divide it by five and then subtract it with the five squares calculation. This will be the extent of your work. Any idea can be carried out in this way.

Most filet crochet patterns only use empty and filled squares. Each mesh is composed of three triple stitches in a row, and an empty stitch contains a pair, each line, then a third.

The difficulty often occurs because you need to note that these meshes are part of a sequence, with the exception of end mesh. Please read the separate article entitled Learning Filet Crochet Patterns for more specific details about a filet crochet map.

If you speak to people about filet crochet, they can use triple stitches and chain stitches for their squares (mesh), while others use double crochet stitches. There is no real difference between any process and any form of stitch you prefer. You may find that when worked with double crochet stitches, the work comes slightly smaller, in a finer mesh or that the meshes created are rectangular.

Any stitch you want to use is very close to the technique and square (mesh) shapes. Replace the double crochet stitch with the trims used in the above pattern. Then use Two chain stitches for empty fabric instead of one for tops and Four double crochet in a row for the filled mesh.

ENJOY LEARNING CROCHET CURTAINS BY YOURSELF

Many people wonder if curtains can be crocheted. Well, the reality is that it is both possible and straightforward. The first thing to do is to mount your curtain rods. Be sure the durable rods are correctly mounted, so the crochet screens are not too noisy. Before beginning, make sure that you decide how long you want them to stay, put the screen rod over the window, etc.

It is crucial that the distance, the diameter of your rod, and storage are measured correctly so that there won't be a mistake further. If the number of panels to be used before you crochet displays are decided, it is necessary to choose the yarn type and backrest. That combination makes the curtain 's aesthetics look impressive. It is your personal preference to select the type of yarn and the backrest. This mixture also depends on your room's color and design.

To crochet curtains, ensure that single stitching is used and blocks with wobble stitches are made. You can pick the length you want and then continue with double crochet stitches. Use the strips to secure the panels around the rims. To connect these panels to the plates, use single stitches. This is a fun-loving experience to crochet curtains rather than relying on a person to do this work. It's a perfect way to add underlying elegance to your home.

CONCLUSION

Crochet is a way to make the beautiful fabric which can be used as curtains, panels, and doilies. The crochet method also helps you to create fashionable winter accessories like hats, mitts, scarves, and some other pieces.

The craft of crocheting has existed since the beginning of 1800, at least. There is some evidence that it existed before, but there seems to be no firm proof of its origin.

You need yarn and a crochet hook to crochet. The crochet is basically a thin stick with a small pointing button (hook) at one end to work the thread over the active loop. Unlike knitting, you usually have just one active loop on your handle, so it's ideal for working with yarn.

You effectively start a crochet project with a slip knot on your ring. Then wrap the yarn over the hook and pull it through the knot. This is also the first chain, and mostly you can create as many as you need to achieve the desired amount of your fabric.

After your chains have been completed, you will start to work directly into the strings in your first section. You just thread the hook into the chain and wrap the yarn around the hook and pull it through the chain stitch to do this. You should have two loops on your hook. To finish the thread, wrap the yarn around the hook and pull it over the two loops once again.

There are also other crochet stitches that you can use similarly to make lovely lace.

You can crochet the work in rows or in circles and work on the previous row or circle. If you work in rows, then at the end of each row, you will switch your work. If you work in circles, a common approach is to add a slip point to each round.

This book is the easiest way to learn is to crochet basic patterns for beginners. Another thing that will help you learn faster is to take a few minutes to get to know the crochet abbreviations and how to read crochet patterns or crochet graphs. Both of them are easy to understand and learning to read them will help you to explore the art of crochet much more quickly.

CPSIA information can be obtained
at www.ICGtesting.com
Printed in the USA
BVHW051645140623
665951BV00002B/9